Political Demonology

Political Demonology

On Modern Marcionism

RICHARD FABER

Translated and Edited by
Therese Feiler and Michael Mayo

CASCADE Books · Eugene, Oregon

POLITICAL DEMONOLOGY
On Modern Marcionism

Copyright © 2018 Richard Faber. All rights reserved. Except for brief quotations in critical publications or reviews, no part of this book may be reproduced in any manner without prior written permission from the publisher. Write: Permissions, Wipf and Stock Publishers, 199 W. 8th Ave., Suite 3, Eugene, OR 97401.

Cascade Books
An Imprint of Wipf and Stock Publishers
199 W. 8th Ave., Suite 3
Eugene, OR 97401

www.wipfandstock.com

PAPERBACK ISBN: 978-1-4982-0129-2
HARDCOVER ISBN: 978-1-4982-8587-2
EBOOK ISBN: 978-1-4982-0130-8

Cataloguing-in-Publication data:

Names: Faber, Richard. | Feiler, Therese, translator and editor. | Mayo, Michael, translator and editor.

Title: Political demonology : on modern Marcionism / Richard Faber ; edited by Therese Feiler and Michael Mayo.

Description: Eugene, OR : Cascade Books, 2018 | Includes bibliographical references.

Identifiers: ISBN 978-1-4982-0129-2 (paperback) | ISBN 978-1-4982-8587-2 (hardcover) | ISBN 978-1-4982-0130-8 (ebook)

Subjects: LCSH: Marcion, of Sinope, active 2nd century. | Auerbach, Erich, 1892–1957. | Bloch, Ernst, 1885–1977. Atheismus im Christentum. | Schmitt, Carl, 1888–1985. | Gnosticism. | Religion and literature. | Religion and sociology. | Church and state—Catholic Church.

Classification: BT1415 .F33 2018 (paperback) | BT1415 .F33 (ebook)

Manufactured in the U.S.A.   12/18/17

Translation supported by Kunststiftung Sachsen-Anhalt, Germany

KUNSTSTIFTUNG
         SACHSEN-ANHALT

Original publication: Richard Faber, *Politische Dämonologie: Über modernen Marcionismus* © Verlag Königshausen & Neumann GmbH, D-Würzburg 2006

Excursus I original publication: Richard Faber, "Nemo contra deum nisi deus ipse": Gegen Hans Blumenbergs Politische Polytheologie", Teil B in: *Der Prometheus-Komplex. Zur Kritik der Politotheologie Eric Voegelins und Hans Blumenbergs* © Verlag Königshausen & Neumann GmbH, D-Würzburg 1984

Excursus II original publication: Richard Faber, 'Der Hahn', in: *Die besten Nebenrollen. 50 Porträts biblischer Randfiguren*, ed. by Marion Keuchen, Helga Kuhlmann, Harald Schroeter-Wittke © Evangelische Verlagsanstalt GmbH, Leipzig 2006

Contents

Translators' Introduction | vii
Preface | xxi

I *Humilitas qua Sublimitas:* Erich Auerbach's Sociology of Literary Religion in the Context of Modern Marcionism | 1
  1. Auerbach, Bloch, and Taubes | 1
  2. Auerbach and Adorno | 18

II Atheism in Christianity—Christianity in Atheism: Ernst Bloch's Revolutionary Marcionism | 29
  1. A Polar Differentiation in the Concept of Atheism | 29
  2. Not a Neo-Paganism | 32
  3. A Humanist, Materialist, and Socialist Atheism | 36
  4. Social-Revolutionary Judaism and Christianity | 41
  5. Modern Marcionism | 49
  6. Atheism in Heretical Christianity and Christianity in Revised Marxism | 54
  7. Meta-Enlightenment | 57
  8. Utopian and Militant This-Worldliness | 61
  9. The Optimism of a Realist | 64

III Political Demonology: On the Counter-Revolutionary Marcionism of Carl Schmitt and Others | 69
  Introduction | 69
  1. The Counter-Revolutionary Apocalypticism of Donoso Cortés and Carl Schmitt | 73
  2. The Roman Catholic and Roman-Atheist Counter-Revolution, Especially Charles Mauras's | 79
  3. Euhemeristic Theism, or Rather: Catholic Atheism | 86

4. Church-State Dualism | 92
5. A Permanent Katechontic as much as Augustan State of Siege | 96
6. Pro-Roman Anti-Judaism and Anti-Christianity, in Particular Carl Schmitt's | 99

Excursus I
"Nemo contra deum nisi deus ipse": Against Hans Blumenberg's Political Poly-Theology | 105

Excursus II
The Cock: *A contribution to the political-theological heraldry of the Bible and its re-writings* | 117

Translators' Introduction

Political demonology has traditionally related to the "experience of evil principalities and powers (of a personal kind) in the world," as the Catholic theologian Karl Rahner explains, but is "not in itself primarily a real revelation." Demonology allows us to seek out and determine the nature of evil, but, despite whatever satisfactions it may bring, does not concern revelation in itself. Instead, as Rahner argues, a powerful yet not real experience of political evil could form "part of the critical context of the real revelation of the living God in Christ and his power to redeem man." So for Christian theology, demons—political or otherwise—are made meaningful in the context of Christ's revelation, which allows this experience of evil to be defined, delimited, and understood.[1]

Most of the thinkers appearing in this volume are hardly regarded as theologians. Carl Schmitt, Ernst Bloch, Theodor Adorno, and Hans Blumenberg, for example, reflected on and critically intervened in the "demonic" experiences of twentieth-century Germany as political, philosophical, legal thinkers. Richard Faber's study, however, reconstructs their thought in light of what he sees as its implicit "demonological" dimensions. No matter how unorthodox, implicit, or marginal the theology they imply, Faber is acutely aware of its practical, political significance. Nothing less than the nature of the political order, and therefore also the dynamics of good and evil, is at stake. Is this order dualistic, marked by enmity? If so, who stands opposed to whom? Is it monistic, implying a single leader or "Führer"? Or does it resolve into the pluralism of the many, to the point of competitive oligarchy, or perhaps into late-capitalist, atomistic competition?

---

1. Karl Rahner, "Demonology," *Encyclopedia of Theology* (London: Burns & Oates, 1975), 333–34.

Translators' Introduction

For Faber, all political constellations and events—the Roman Empire, Christendom, the French and American revolutions, postwar Europe—are also irreducibly religious constellations. And as such they pervade culture and politics today. As Faber's multidisciplinary approach recalls and reinterprets these constellations in the tradition of the Frankfurt Institut für Sozialforschung, he uses his objects "like spotlights" to critically illuminate the present.[2]

HARNACK'S MARCION

But what is the role of Marcion here, the second-century arch-heretic? The study of gnosis,[3] Faber's teacher Jacob Taubes once remarked, has primarily referred to the gnosis of late antiquity. "[But] palimpsestically," he wrote, "it can also be read as the self-localization of the present."[4] And when Adolf von Harnack published his study of Marcion in 1921, it was not merely a work of church history. Understood as instrumental in the very foundation of the Catholic Church—as Harnack's subtitle, "The Gospel of the Alien God," suggests—Marcion was a *figura* to locate liberal Protestant faith after the First World War.[5] Like few other figures in the history of the church, Marcion articulated the possibility of dualism—of total otherness—within Christianity itself.[6] He taught an altogether new God revealed by Christ, one that negated the old god of the Jews—and with him all creation. At

---

2. Christine Holste, "Einleitung," in *A propos: kulturwissenschaftliche Miszellen von und für Richard Faber*, edited by Christine Holste and Barbara von Reibnitz (Würzburg: Königshausen & Neumann, 2013), 15.

3. NB: Marcion grounds his thoughts fully in emergent the New Testament, but shares the characteristic gnostic dualism and certainly had ties with the Syrian Gnostic Cerdo, cf. Adolf von Harnack, *Marcion, Das Evangelium vom fremden Gott: Eine Monographie zur Geschichte der Grundlegung der Katholischen Kirche* (Leipzig: Hinrichs'sche Buchhandlung, 1921), 26; Barbara Aland, *Die Gnosis* (Stuttgart: Reclam, 2014).

4. Jacob Taubes, "Einleitung: Das stählerne Gehäuse und der Exodus daraus oder ein Streit um Marcion, einst und heute," in *Gnosis und Politik*, edited by Jacob Taubes (Munich: Wilhelm Fink, 1984), 9.

5. Harnack, *Marcion*, 28; Wolfram Kinzig, *Harnack, Marcion und das Judentum* (Leipzig: Evangelische Verlags-Anstalt, 2004), 109.

6. The evaluation of this "within" is currently shifting, giving Marcion a constructive role beyond the dialectical negative, e.g., Jürgen Regul, "Die Bedeutung Marcions aus der Sicht heutiger kirchlicher Praxis," in *Marcion und seine kirchengeschichtliche Wirkung/Marcion and His Impact on Church History*, edited by Martin Meiser (Berlin: de Gruyter, 2002), 293–312.

Translators' Introduction

the same time, this new god was nothing but goodness itself, all-merciful love, indeed unspeakably so: "Oh what wonder above wonder, what delight, power, and astonishment it is that nothing can be said about the gospel, nor thought about it, nor can it be compared to anything."[7] Faith sprung from a great Beyond, the altogether New that denied a world in shell shock. As Harnack's daughter and biographer Agnes von Zahn-Harnack explained,

> Marcion preached "the alien God," i.e., the God that has nothing in common with creation, this miserable, misconceived, and stained creation, and the whole course of earthly events, because he belongs to a wholly different sphere. This was bound to deeply move readers for whom, through war and revolution, the cruelty, the counter-divine meaninglessness of fate, had become a horrific experience. Yet at the same time Marcion taught the coming of the Redeemer, who is perfect love and nothing but love; no more punitive justice, no more legality![8]

The unbridgeable division between the old creator and that new, pure god of love implied an irreconcilable fissure—for good or ill.

As Harnack told it, Marcion (ca. 85–160) was a bishop's son in the Pontus, born into a lively Christian community. His own father excommunicated him, though probably not because he had seduced a virgin. Christianity at the time was still in its formative years, so only severely deviant doctrines would have led to excommunication. Marcion's unforgiveable teaching of two gods, Harnack argued, must have been quite developed when he left the Pontus for a "propaganda tour" of Asia Minor.[9] It was most likely here that he encountered Polycarp, who, as Irenaeus of Lyon writes, said to Marcion, "I recognize you as the first-born of Satan"—indeed, a demon.

The merchant Marcion headed on to Rome, the epicenter from which new ideas would ripple throughout the empire. Here he collated an *Evangelion*, a version of Luke's Gospel the early church came to regard as a mutilation (a view recently revised, albeit only on the grounds of historical accuracy).[10] Marcion's *Apostolikon* was comprised of ten letters of

---

7. Harnack, *Marcion*, 158.

8. Cited in Karl-Heinz Menke, *Spielarten des Marcionismus in der Geistesgeschichte des 20. Jahrhunderts*, ed. Nordrhein-Westfälische Akademie der Wissenschaften und der Künste (Paderborn: Ferdinand Schöningh, 2011), 10. This work was partly inspired by the present volume.

9. Harnack, *Marcion*, 22.

10. Dieter T. Roth, *The Text of Marcion's Gospel* (Boston: Brill, 2015), 7–45.

Paul, though now stripped of all Jewish material. The collation served one purpose: to show that the new god of pure love had overthrown the old. The Old Testament was obsolete. Around AD 144, still in Rome, Marcion composed his infamous *Antitheses*, surviving only within the scathing polemics written against him. As the title suggests, the *Antitheses* are a sharp juxtaposition of the inferior world-creator and the good God, or rather his Christ.[11]

The Roman presbyters met Marcion's *Antitheses* with hostility. Their "pluralistic tolerance scheme," as Sebastian Moll has called it, could absorb all diversities—except those questioning that tolerance scheme itself. For founding his "anti-movement" Marcion was once again excommunicated.[12] But this time, "with monstrous energy, Marcion suffered the consequence, and began his Reformatory propaganda at the grandest scale," and his church spread throughout the empire.[13] Even a generation later, Tertullian, his fiercest theological opponent, warned, "Marcion's heretical tradition has filled the whole world" (*Adversus Marcionem* V, 19). Long after his church had disappeared, "Marcion" signified a taboo, an abyss within the church. As Catholic orthodoxy took shape in response to Marcion, this abyssal logic—a logic of opposition, of antithesis and internal contradiction—persisted, not just as a theological possibility, but as political and cultural possibilities as well.

MODERN MARCIONISM

For Harnack, in his first, prize-winning study of the subject in 1871, Marcion's absolutized dichotomy between law and gospel prefigured the Reformation's irreversible breakup of the church.[14] Christ stood against a demiurgic creator and his world, a "bad tree" that produced nothing but bad fruit. The new, revealed God set Christ against Yahweh, the gospel against Judaism, and—in Harnack's analogy—the Reformation against the Roman Catholic Church. Marcion was Luther. This "emphasis on Marcion's 'undogmatic way of thinking'" could then be extended into the twentieth

---

11. Harnack, *Marcion*, 24, 69.

12. Sebastian Moll, *The Arch-Heretic Marcion* (Tübingen: Mohr Siebeck, 2010), 44, 125.

13. Harnack, *Marcion*, 25.

14. Adolf von Harnack, *Die Dorpater Preisschrift: Der erste Reformator*, edited by Friedemann Steck (Berlin: de Gruyter, 2003); cf. Kinzig, *Harnack*, 107, 145.

century. For one thing, it allowed Harnack to subtly resist "the dogmatism of the Prussian state church."¹⁵ But Harnack also saw in Marcion a genuine dimension of orthodoxy. In a letter to Martin Rade just after the publication of *Marcion*, Harnack wrote, ". . . it was my intention to pay what is due to Marcion in church history at last . . . The place he deserves should become clear: Between Paul and Augustine he was the most important Christian."¹⁶ For Harnack, dualism and orthodoxy could come together in one Christian heart.

A prolific church historian and editor since his early days in Estonia, Harnack had risen to the highest ranks of the Wilhelmine Reich's academic elite. A member of the Prussian Academy of Science, he became general director of the Prussian State Library in 1905. Six years later he cofounded the Kaiser Wilhelm Society for the Advancement of the Sciences. The subliminal dualism that fascinated Harnack's enlightened, liberal Protestantism also echoed in his advocacy of Germany's foreign policy. In August 1914 he shared in the national enthusiasm of the "August Experience" as Germany declared war against France and Russia. He did not only perceive it as a *bellum iustum*. He was not shy about attaching the title "Prince of Peace"¹⁷ to the sovereign. The whole German populace, he wrote, "gives its last drop of blood [to Your Majesty]; the furor teutonicus breaks loose with all its might, and not a single one will stay behind!" This was a "war of minds," a *Kulturkampf*, indeed a clash of civilizations. As one of the signatories of the so-called Manifesto of the Ninety-Three in October 1914, Harnack defended Germany's invasion of Belgium, the country's "hard struggle for existence in a struggle which has been forced upon her."¹⁸

As a religious-philosophical constellation, Marcionism entailed a remarkable dialectic of liberalism¹⁹ and anti-Judaism. Harnack concluded

---

15. Kinzig, *Harnack*, 145.

16. Harnack to Rade, 28.12.1920 [original emphasis], cited in Kinzig, *Harnack*, 74.

17. Christian Nottmeier, *Adolf von Harnack und die deutsche Politik 1890–1930* (Tübingen: Mohr Siebeck, 2004), 379.

18. Professors of Germany, "To the Civilized World," *The North American Review* 210, No. 765 (August 1919), 284–87, 284. Harnack later claimed he had supported the document without knowing its exact wording. See Nottmeier, *Harnack und die deutsche Politik*, 390.

19. According to Martin Rumscheidt, Harnack's liberalism was liberal in the deepest sense: a theology committed to the freedom of thought, confident in the human spirit, believing in the power of reason in search for objective truth. And an "inseparable component of that freedom for both [Harnack and Bonhoeffer] was a clear grasp of social and political freedom." Martin Rumscheidt, "The Significance of Adolf von Harnack

that "[to] discard the Old Testament in the second century was a mistake that the great Church was right to reject; to hold on to it in the sixteenth century was a fate the Reformation could not yet escape; but to keep on conserving it as a canonical work in Protestantism since the nineteenth century is the result of a religious and ecclesial paralysis."[20] This last consequence darkly foreshadowed statements such as Cardinal Faulhaber's in 1933 that a "Christianity which still clings to the Old Testament is a Jewish religion, irreconcilable with the spirit of the German people." Harnack's theological influence waned during the 1920s, so the later rise of anti-Semitism cannot be laid at his feet. In 1924, in fact, he had warned, "One ought not to imagine that the ravages of our time can be healed with parades, swastikas, and steel-helmets."[21] It would be difficult and anachronistic to draw a straight line from his study of Marcion to the *völkisch* German Church of the Nazi era.[22] Nonetheless, Harnack's challenge, Marcion's question—what to do with the Old Testament, and therefore with the world and with the political—continues to blight liberal Protestantism to this day.[23]

RICHARD FABER'S PROJECT

The key date for *Political Demonology* is 1968, the height of the German postwar generation's autopsy of their parents' totalitarianism. As a child of this "protest generation," Richard Faber has pursued two interrelated lines of enquiry: the dissection of fascism and the unmasking of theocracy in its various forms and intellectual trajectories. Fascism and theocracy are, for Faber, conceptually inseparable. Whenever it invokes unity or the whole,

---

and Reinhold Seeberg for Dietrich Bonhoeffer," in *Bonhoeffer's Intellectual Formation: Theology and Philosophy in His Thought*, edited by Peter Frick (Tübingen: Mohr Siebeck), 201–24, 212.

20. Harnack, *Marcion*, 249.
21. Cited in Rumscheidt, "The Significance of Adolf von Harnack," 212.
22. Kinzig, *Harnack*, 109, 144.
23. Cf. the scandal around the Old Testament scholar Notger Slenczka in 2015, see e.g., Reinhard Bingener, "Der Gott des Gemetzels," *Frankfurter Allgemeine Zeitung*, 21.04.2015, http://www.faz.net/aktuell/politik/inland/berlin-professor-fordert-abschaffung-des-alten-testaments-13549027.html#lesermeinungen; and the charge of Marcionism against the former German Evangelical-Lutheran bishop Margot Käßmann in 2016: Hannes Stein, "Käßmanns Pazifismus ist vor allem eines—nicht christlich," *Die Welt*, 31.03.2016, http://www.welt.de/debatte/kommentare/article153862512/Kaessmanns-Pazifismus-ist-vor-allem-eines-nicht-christlich.html.

Translators' Introduction

the amalgamation of politics and religion can always only birth immanent, ultimately collectivist institutions.[24] But such institutions necessarily also produce a historical, logical excess: the survivors of totalitarianism, the militant resistance, the traumatized, the melancholics—and not least: religio-political heretics. It was also in 1968 that a Marcionite constellation seemed to have re-emerged in West Germany. On the one hand stood the activists inspired by the Frankfurt School, especially Adorno, who spoke from the self-defeating movement of critique, the only negative truth left to utter in this "damaged life."[25] On the other hand stood the establishment with its various ties to the fascist era, but also to anti-revolutionary traditions, conservative stability, and at times monarchist ideas of order.

THEOCRACY—IMPERIALISM—FASCISM

This German constellation forms the background to Faber's critical fascination with Carl Schmitt, whom he has aptly called "the theologian of jurisprudence and the jurist of theology."[26] Faber argues that Schmitt's Prussian heritage had far less of an influence on his political theology than did his Roman Catholicism.[27] Yet Schmitt was a Roman before he was a Catholic. The Roman emperors served as a lens for his political Catholicism, not vice versa: as the divinely guaranteed juridical form; a singular divine leader holding back the dissolutions of republican anarchy, or indeed any threats associated with divided power.[28] In other words, what is at stake is not whether Schmitt was a theologian or not, but rather: Which theo-political order did he proclaim? Schmitt knew Harnack's study of Marcion well and revived the theological heritage once again as a lever to distribute the powers of the present. In Schmitt's reading, a pagan but effective monotheism governed the imperial cult of Augustus, then found a seamless continuation

---

24. See, especially, Richard Faber, *Wir sind Eins: Über politisch-religiöse Ganzheitsvorstellungen europäischer Faschismen* (Würzburg: Königshausen & Neumann, 2005).

25. Cf. Theodor W. Adorno, *Minima Moralia: Reflections from Damaged Life*, translated by E. F. N. Jephcott (London: Verso, 2005).

26. Richard Faber, *Lateinischer Faschismus: Über Carl Schmitt den Römer und Katholiken* (Berlin: Philo, 2001).

27. Even though by no means in the majority, Faber's own alternative leftwing Catholicism during the 1960s highlights the unabated religious and theological dimension of postwar political discourse in Germany.

28. Schmitt, for his part, criticized Faber's "anti-Roman affect." Faber, *Lateinischer Faschismus*, 12 n. 17.

Translators' Introduction

in the Christianization of the Roman Empire (which Faber for his part interprets as the imperialization and paganization of Christianity). Finally, the katechontic constellation returns in the strictly "monotheistic" order of a *Führer*, as Faber frequently emphasizes. As late as 1970 in *Political Theology II*, Schmitt explained—with reference to the imperial theologian Eusebius and the rebellious monks in the Eastern Roman Empire—that the static nature of monotheism simultaneously implies *stasis* and *therefore* upheaval. The in-breaking messianic harbors the dissolution of "all that stands and all the estates," to translate Marx correctly here. Political Christology for Schmitt, in Faber's reading, thus implied routing out dissent—political demonology.

So the total, even totalitarian religious-political "wholes" of Western modernity find their original image in the Roman Empire, this ancient prototype of "Euro-American empire." Rome is the mother of the Occident and its ideology: "Whoever says Occident is searching for the inheritance deed of the Roman Empire."[29] It is also no coincidence, Faber points out, that the *novus ordo seclorum* announced on the Great Seal of the U.S. draws on the imperial Roman poet Vergil's fourth *Eclogue*. An essential line of enquiry into the study of political religion thus also has to examine the modern reception of Roman antiquity.[30]

Distinctions need to be made here as well, Faber has argued: a Neo-Kantian, liberating humanism can be harnessed to an emancipatory project, unlike what he calls a Caesarist, aristocratic, effectively anti-humanist humanism. (The nineteenth-century bourgeois middle class reading Greek and Latin could very well produce a Heinrich Himmler, after all.) Notably, this anti-humanist tradition continues well into the postmodern era: for example, in Foucault's idea of the subject that truly becomes himself only by virtue of his own disappearance.[31]

---

29. Reinhold Schneider cited in Richard Faber, *Abendland: Ein politischer Kampfbegriff*, 2nd ed. (Berlin: Philo, 2002), 96.

30. *Antike heute*, edited by Richard Faber and Bernhard Kytzler (Würzburg: Königshausen & Neumann, 1992); there also Faber, "Vergil nach Auschwitz. Zum 100. Geburtstag von Ludwig Strauß," 197–215.

31. Richard Faber, "Humanistische und faschistische Welt. Über Ludwig Curtius (1874–1954)," in *Streit um den Humanismus*, edited by Richard Faber (Würzburg: Königshausen & Neumann, 2003), 17–18.

Translators' Introduction

THE "DEMONIC" AND REVOLUTIONARY HOPE

Interpreting Christ as a political revolutionary has always been a heady possibility, as old as the gospels themselves. In the modern age of revolutions, Christ the revolutionary reappeared. Whether as a sans-culotte, as the Promethean thought of the Enlightenment, or as the silent force of subversion in Dostoevsky's "Grand Inquisitor"—such insurgents challenged both material politics and a particular notion of orthodox, Trinitarian Christianity, subjecting them to a logic of opposition between Two. In its most radical expression, this insurgency becomes an exodus from religion itself, as Faber reconstructs it in Ernst Bloch (see Part II of this volume). Bloch's chief argument is one of immanence—of utopia within the material world. His utopia places human non-finitude and human material reality at the center. In the very loss of the transcendent possibilities offered by traditional religion, the non-finality of the human allows us to nonetheless hope for a Marcionite Other, a "transcending without transcendence." Christianity contains within itself the means of its own overcoming: it extends the Exodus, its earthly demand for justice for the poor and oppressed, its anti-authoritarianism. A non-transcendent Christianity that has such "atheism" within it is heretical, of course, and Bloch embraces this fact. ("The best thing about religion is that it creates heretics," he writes.) But Christianity is required nonetheless. It saves atheism from becoming a brute materialism (*Klotzmaterialismus*), nihilism, and despondent boredom.

Reading the New Testament alongside Marx, Bloch accepted the "metaphysical anti-Semitism" his anti-theocratic quest implied. An underlying current of the ongoing debate around the figure of Marcion thus also concerns the religio-political interpretation of Israel. Another dualist Either/Or can emerge here: either one has to embrace a "theocratic" connection of Judaism and nationalism, or an exodus to the point of atheism, albeit with Haredi Judaism as a (negativized) possibility. The emphatic Israeli then paradoxically finds himself without a home. Jewish contemporaries such as Will Self and Shlomo Sand engage in this debate. An Israeli with a universalist horizon, Sand scourges Judaism as much as nationalism, which he thinks are inextricably, inescapably intertwined—to the detriment of peace in Israel. But neither does he give a break to secular Judaism. And in denying that such a thing exists, the atheist Sand even more emphatically embraces a deeply orthodox notion of Judaism.[32]

32. Shlomo Sand, *How I Stopped Being a Jew* (London: Verso, 2014); Will Self, "How

Translators' Introduction

A curious dialectic also underlies the coherence of Faber's essays in this volume. Marcion(ism)'s dualistic mode of existence leaves the Old and New as open, interchangeable, though always inimical spaces. Judaism could stand for the Old, indeed all worldly existence, to be abandoned, ascetically or violently; it could be the dangerous "New" flying the flags of revolution. "Judaeo-Christianity" could threaten an anti-Marcionite paganism; Jesus could be the Jewish insurgent against a Jewish establishment aligned with Roman imperialism. In this sense Schmitt always argued that the "right" and "left" are two sides of the same coin. But while Jacob Taubes pressed Schmitt on his connection with Walter Benjamin,[33] Faber for his part has emphasized their significant distance: "Schmitt was a Christologist in the sense of Th. Hobbes: 'Jesus is the Christ,' i.e.: the Messiah is (and has long been) here; hence every messianism (no matter which form) is heresy/revolution, which must be fought. Benjamin, in contrast, was a messianic par excellence, the very opposite of a 'katechontic.' His 'Antichrist' is not to be restrained, but rather to be fought and vanquished—for the sake of the Messiah..."[34]

The first chapter of *Political Demonology*, a study of the Jewish literary critic Erich Auerbach (1892–1957), perhaps surprises with its reference to Marcionism. Auerbach, as Faber admits, mentions Harnack, but never Marcion. What counts is rather the constellation, the ache and longing for something alien, unreachable—a god, a home—that imbues Auerbach's work with existential intensity. For the Jewish Auerbach, to put it "christologically," the divine is incarnate in historical and above all literary reality. In this religious intensity, literary reality combines the tragic and the comic, the most quotidian and the sublime. It is a living reality throughout the

---

I Stopped Being a Jew by Shlomo Sand; and *Unchosen: The Memoirs of a Philo-Semite* by Julie Burchill—review," *The Guardian*, 06 Nov 2014; similarly Yascha Mounk, *Echt, du bist Jude?—Fremd im eigenen Land* (Zürich: Kein & Aber, 2015). For a veritable Marxist-atheist *resurrection*, see Will Self's "The North London Book of the Dead" in the short story collection *The Quantity Theory of Insanity* (London: Bloomsbury, 1991). Will Self's exploration of Bristol's labyrinthine concrete landscapes significantly echoes Walter Benjamin. In twentieth-century Germany Faber observed a similar constellation through the "antipodes" Hans-Joachim Schoeps and Jacob Taubes. See Richard Faber, *Deutschbewusstes Judentum und jüdischbewusstes Deutschtum—Der Historische und Politische Theologe Hans-Joachim Schoeps* (Würzburg: Königshausen & Neumann, 2008).

33. *Jacob Taubes—Carl Schmitt: Briefwechsel mit Materialien*, edited by Herbert Kopp-Oberstebrink, Thorsten Palzhoff and Martin Treml (Munich: Wilhelm Fink, 2011), 29.

34. Personal message to the translators.

Translators' Introduction

ages, and hence includes biblical as well as "profane" literature. As Arthur Krystal puts it, "For Auerbach, a philologist by training, but a historian-philosopher by temperament, literature is always bounded by the writer's sense of reality, which, at its deepest level, depicts everyday life in all its seriousness."[35] Although monumental in its own right, Auerbach's work was also a spotlight on his political context. In 1938 he writes to Traugott Fuchs with a view to fascist Germany:

> The challenge is not to grasp and digest all the evil that's happening—that's not too difficult—but much more to find a point of departure for those historical forces that can be set against it ... To seek for them in myself, to track them down in the world, completely absorbs me. The old forces of resistance—churches, democracies, education, economic laws—are useful and effective only if they are renewed and activated through a new force not yet visible to me.

As Krystal further notes, "[that] new force never emerged, and Auerbach could never take solace in the future." He remained an exile in more than one sense, "a Jew outside of Judaism and a German ousted from Germany." Apart from the bond of friendship between Auerbach and Ernst Bloch, this background further adds to the "neo-marcionite" dimension Faber explores in his first chapter.

Auerbach's fate as an exile in the U.S. is then echoed in the Excursuses, two earlier publications Faber has included in this volume with a view to an American audience. The first is a rejection of the "poly-theological" solution to theodicy suggested by Hans Blumenberg and others against Carl Schmitt; Faber defends once again a Blochian, utopian-revolutionary position. This chapter in particular participates in contemporary debates, as it asks us to critically examine whether the argument for pluralism is actually a mask to promote oligarchic and plutocratic interests.

The second Excursus retraces the Marcionite dimension in Herman Melville as it moved between revolutionary hope and its disappointment in the face of reality; of particular note will be its introductory poem "The Cock" by Christian Morgenstern, translated into English here for the first time.

---

35. Arthur Krystal, "The Book of Books: Erich Auerbach and the Making of 'Mimesis,'" *The New Yorker,* December 9, 2013, http://www.newyorker.com/magazine/2013/12/09/the-book-of-books.

Translators' Introduction

HOPE FULFILLED?

Just as the Burning Man Festival is now the playground of billionaires, the subversive impulse of the 1960s was absorbed by the establishment. Today, for many, the socialist revolution in the West seems frozen in time, like a prehistoric insect encapsulated in amber. Dialectically, of course, this potential is resurfacing elsewhere. But for his part Faber finds a path for the fulfillment of revolutionary Marcionite hopes beyond the Marcionite-theocratic dialectic in the figure of the cosmopolitan humanist. In this respect he has revisited many key figures in the tradition: Dante Alighieri, the proto-humanist and tragic exile from Florence; Erasmus of Rotterdam; Thomas Mann; the humanist historian Friedrich Heer; and even across the Atlantic, Susan Sontag, who was, like Faber, a student of Jacob Taubes.[36] For her part Sontag was a great connoisseur of gnosis. This impulse culminated in aesthetic fascination—though perpetually struggling against fascist aesthetics. Faber keenly admires her "universalist" perspective: anti-gnostic, but not submitting to the theocratic.[37] And it was from her enlightened cosmopolitan perspective that Sontag always championed a better, a true America: it could be the heir of a true, enlightened, humanist Europe—again an unabashedly utopian project.

A NOTE ON METHOD AND TRANSLATION

Political Demonology is an homage to Harnack, but its academic method is deeply indebted to Walter Benjamin and the Frankfurt School. Faber interprets his material through meticulous collection and collation, through association, parenthesis, and paradox. He creates a mosaic of heavily punctuated cross-references, self-quotations, and repetitions, even collages within collages. At times his own voice seems to disappear in this process. Indeed, as one critic wrote, "with the author no more than a conférencier, who only leads over from one quotation to another, the file card box itself seems to speak."[38] Faber consciously seeks to shatter the dogmatic edifice academic truth-claims often make. Its quotation-shards then serve to re-

---

36. Faber, *Avancierte Ästhetin und politische Moralistin: Die universelle Intellektuelle Susan Sontag* (Würzburg: Königshausen & Neumann, 2006).

37. Susan Sontag, "Fascinating Fascism," *New York Review of Books*, February 6, 1975.

38. Michael Wetzel, "Der von Göttern du stammst: Richard Faber weiß, wo es mit Goethe endet," *Frankfurter Allgemeine Zeitung*, http://www.faz.net/aktuell/feuilleton/buecher/rezension-sachbuch-der-von-goettern-du-stammst-11307169-p2.html

Translators' Introduction

construct a more brittle, more accurate representation of absolute truth: as the very denial to represent what cannot be represented.[39] This is no less morally authoritative and urgent; quite the opposite. It is also an invitation to join Faber to "write further" and participate in the contested cultural narratives that have been alive throughout the centuries.

As always, much gets lost in translation. Most noteworthy is the word *Reich*, upon which the divergent implications in the text hangs: it is used for Empire, the Third Reich, and the Kingdom (of God). Many particles used in the German had to be left untranslated so as to make the text more accessible. Nonetheless, wherever possible we have tried to convey the density and complexity of Faber's original. Wherever he has inserted words into his quotations, we put them in square brackets without further reference; any German words in square brackets are those of the original. Translators' footnotes are marked with an asterisk.

Our thanks go to Alexander Breton for his help with the French sections, and to the Faculty of Theology and Religion at Oxford for supporting the Political Demonology Working Group in Trinity Term 2016. We are particularly grateful to the Kunststiftung Sachsen-Anhalt (Germany), who granted a work stipend to Therese Feiler for this project in 2015; and last but not least we thank Richard Faber for his helpful comments and additional materials.

T.F. and M.M.
Oxford, Michaelmas 2017

---

39. Richard Faber, *Der Collage-Essay. Eine wissenschaftliche Darstellungsform. Hommage à Walter Benjamin* (Hildesheim: Gerstenberg, 1979).

Preface

The three self-standing parts of this book were all written in 2004, though my engagement with these topics goes back to the late 1960s. The obvious cut-off date is 1968; besides everything else, this year saw Ernst Bloch's *Atheism in Christianity* published (and immediately read by me), and my final studies at the Freie Universität began—most significantly with Jacob Taubes. Down to the subtitles these three studies are indebted to this philosopher and sociologist of religion from Berlin; but also to Erich Auerbach, whom he held in highest esteem; as well as to Theodor W. Adorno, who again and again challenged Taubes; and to Ernst Bloch. I had heard this last already in 1963-64 during my first semester at Tübingen and have remained wholly influenced by him.[40] I obtained my doctorate, however, with a dissertation on Carl Schmitt, albeit a critical one. It had long been my intention to show that Schmitt's political theology and that of his

---

40. Cf. mainly: *Novalis: Die Phantasie an die Macht* (Stuttgart: Metzler, 1970); *Erbschaft jener Zeit: Zu Ernst Bloch und Hermann Broch* (Würzburg: Königshausen &Neumann, 1989); "Politische Theologie oder: Was heißt Theokratie?," in *Politische Religion—religiöse Politik*, edited by Richard Faber (Würzburg: Königshausen & Neumann, 1997), 19-41; "Politischer Idyllismus in Antike und Moderne," in *Ästhetik des Politischen—Politik des Ästhetischen*, edited by Karlheinz Barck and Richard Faber (Würzburg: Königshausen & Neumann, 1999), 249-71; "Ernst Bloch und das Hambacher 'Fest der Hoffnung,'" in *Liberalismus in Geschichte und Gegenwart*, edited by Richard Faber (Würzburg: Königshausen & Neumann, 2000), 21-37; "'Mit uns zieht die neue Zeit.' Differenzierungen in der Kategorie 'Novum,'" in *Säkularisierung und Resakralisierung: Zur Geschichte des Kirchenlieds und seiner Rezeption*, edited by Richard Faber (Würzburg: Königshausen & Neumann, 2001), 189-98; Richard Faber, "Ludwigshafen-Mannheim, Munich, Berlin und andernorts: Zur Kulturgeographie der Ernst Blochschen 'Spuren,'" in *Bloch-Jahrbuch* 2006, 111-51; "Revolutionärer Messianismus, moderner Marcionismus und militanter Optimismus: Zu Ernst Blochs allegorischer Markprosa," in *Spuren. Lektüren*, edited by Elmar Locher (Bozen: Studien-Verlag, Edition Sturzflüge, 2008), 25-45.

ideological relatives is essentially political demonology and hence *counter-revolutionary* Marcionism. The dissertation had critically reconstructed the tradition of political theology from Varro and Vergil, via Eusebius and Dante, up to Thomas Hobbes, Donoso Cortés, and Carl Schmitt, the last being the guiding thread.[41]

The year 2004 gave me a good opportunity to finally realize this old plan, because it required two commissioned works from me: a contribution to the Erich-Auerbach-Colloquium at the Berlin Literaturforschungszentrum on the occasion of the seventieth birthday of my friend Karlheinz Barck,[42] a scholar of Romance languages and literatures. And it required from me a lecture in the university lecture series "The Opposite of Belief? Atheism in Discussion,"[43] organized by the Religious Studies scholar Susanne Lanwerd and me during the summer semester at the Freie Universität Berlin. From the first moments of the planning phase, I was determined to lecture on Bloch's *Atheism in Christianity* and to accentuate his revolutionary neo-Marcionism,[44] placing it, to an extent, eye-to-eye with the counter-revolutionary Carl Schmitt. After I had also contextualized Auerbach's "sermo humilis" (following in Taubes's and Adorno's footsteps) as neo-Marcionite, the obvious thing was to unite the three essays into a book: beginning with the one on Auerbach in the field of sociology of *literary* religion, followed by the one on "Atheism in Christianity—Christianity in Atheism" in the field of the philosophy *of religion*, and crowned by the one on the counter-revolutionary demonology of Carl Schmitt and his ideological relatives in the field of the *political science* of religion.

It should be self-evident that certain overlaps were unavoidable. The desired complementarity of the contributions required almost minimal repetition. At the same time these repetitions allow for the sections to be read independently. They "stand" by all means "in themselves."

---

41. Cf. Richard Faber, *Die Verkündigung Vergils: Reich—Kirche—Staat: Zur Kritik der "Politischen Theologie"* (Hildesheim/New York: Olms, 1975).

42. The Erich-Auerbach-Colloquium is documented in the collection *Erich Auerbach: Geschichte und Aktualität eines europäischen Philologen*, edited by Martin Treml and Karlheinz Barck (Berlin: Kulturverlag Kadmos, 2007).

43. The university lectures are documented in the collection: *Atheismus: Ideologie, Philosophie oder Mentalität?*, edited by Richard Faber and Susanne Lanwerd (Würzburg: Königshausen & Neumann, 2006).

44. This accentuation particularly distinguishes my interpretation from the last one—up to 2007—presented by a theologian; cf. Jürgen Moltmann, "Ernst Blochs Christologie," in *Bloch-Almanach* 23/2004, 121f.

Preface

I thank the friends to whom I am indebted apart from the direct and indirect teachers just mentioned, however diverse their attitudes towards (modern) Marcion(ism) may be: the late Siegfried Detemple, Jürgen Ebach, Helge Høibraaten, Martin Leutzsch, Thomas Macho, and Thomas Ruster, but above all the late Carsten Colpe, who with Taubes was the examiner of my dissertation and who—for decades—was one of the most highly regarded specialists on Gnosis in general and Marcion in particular.

Hardly anyone will fail to notice that this book presents not least an homage to Adolf von Harnack's classic "Marcion" study—even though by no means in the vein of the Harnack restoration common today[45]—no matter which part of the book one reads. Altogether, it is a volume on the political[46] history of religion (and the study of it) in the twentieth century, as well as a philological and historical consideration of Auerbach. He was a sociologist of literary *religion*—with a neomarcionite dimension.

---

45. I'm thinking of, for example, *Adolf von Harnack: Theologe, Historiker, Wissenschaftspolitiker*, edited by Kurt Nowak und Otto Gerhard Oexle (Göttingen: Vandenhoeck und Ruprecht, 2001); *Adolf von Harnack: Christentum, Wissenschaft und Gesellschaft*, edited by Kurt Nowak und Otto Gerhard Oexle (Göttingen: Vandenhoeck und Ruprecht, 2003); *Adolf von Harnack: Wesen des Christentums*, ed. and annotated by Trutz Rendtorff (Gütersloh: Kaiser, Gütersloher Verlagshaus, 1999).

46. *Translators' note: The original reads *zur (politologischen) Religionsgeschichte* [on the (politological) history of religion], which partly qualifies Faber's history of religion as "politology," i.e., political science.

1

Humilitas qua Sublimitas
Erich Auerbach's Sociology of Literary Religion in the Context of Modern Marcionism

In memoriam Karlheinz Barck

1. AUERBACH, BLOCH, AND TAUBES

Tolstoy . . . is a Marcionite Christian through and through. The directly religious passages we have from Marcion could well have been written by him, and conversely Marcion would have recognized himself in Tolstoy's "miserable and despised," in his reading of the Sermon on the Mount . . . and in his zeal against common Christendom. On the other hand, Gorky's moving play *The Lower Depths*[1] can be understood as a Marcionite play as well; "The Stranger" who appears here is the Marcionite Christ, and his "Lower Depths" are the world.[2]

1. Translators' note: Gorky's original title is *Na dne—On the Ground*. Translated as *The Lower Depths* in English, it was rendered in German as *Das Nachtasyl* [The Night Asylum], the title Harnack and Faber use.

2. Adolf von Harnack, *Marcion, Das Evangelium vom fremden Gott: Eine Monographie*

Political Demonology

Has Adolf von Harnack, cited here, read Erich Auerbach? Impossible. When the historical theologian Harnack published his masterpiece on Marcion, *The Gospel of the Alien God,* in 1920 (with a revised edition in 1924), nothing relevant was yet available from Auerbach, the scholar of Romance languages and literatures who would later become just as famous as Harnack. But then did Auerbach perhaps study Harnack? Most likely, even though Marcion's name appears in Auerbach's writings only when Auerbach mentions Tertullian's *Adversus Marcionem*.[3] Moreover, Auerbach was a close friend of Ernst Bloch, who had proven to be an excellent reader of Harnack's study of Marcion; Bloch might have even partly inspired Harnack with his work, *The Spirit of Utopia,* dated back in 1918.[4] Like no one else, Bloch—with his Jacob-Taubesian formation of concepts—adhered to a "modern Marcionism."[5] After all, it was Taubes who had explicitly brought Auerbach and Marcion "together" via St. Paul, both with and without Bloch.

These considerations were raised by Ulrich Raulff in the *Süddeutsche Zeitung* in early 2004, when he criticized the German Social Democrats' prevailing discourse on "elitism" and in doing so largely referred to Taubes's "Conversation with Wolfert von Rahden and Norbert Kapferer: Elite or Avant-garde?"[6] This 1982 text was itself initiated by the discourse on

---

zur Geschichte der Grundlegung der katholischen Kirche (Darmstadt: Wissenschaftliche Buchgesellschaft, 1996), 232.

3. Cf. Erich Auerbach, *Gesammelte Aufsätze zur romanischen Philologie* (Bern: Francke, 1967), 65ff.; concerning Harnack in general, see at least Erich Auerbach, *Mimesis: Dargestellte Wirklichkeit in der abendländischen Literatur,* 4th ed. (Bern: Francke, 1967), 45; in the following, "M" will stand for *Mimesis.*

4. With the following words Bloch dedicated a copy of the 2nd edition of 1923 to the couple Erich and Marie Auerbach: "This book . . . for Erich and Marie Auerbach with warm affection as a little wedding torch./ Berlin, 11.6.1923 Ernst Bloch." Cf. *Erich Auerbachs Briefe an Martin Hellweg (1939–1950). Edition und historisch-philologischer Kommentar,* edited by Martin Vialon (Tübingen/Basel: Francke, 1997), 122.

5. Cf. Jacob Taubes, "Walter Benjamin—ein moderner Marcionit? Scholems Benjamin-Interpretation religionsgeschichtlich überprüft," in *Antike und Moderne: Zu Walter Benjamins "Passagen,"* edited by Norbert W. Bolz and Richard Faber (Würzburg: Königshausen & Neumann, 1986), 138–53. Whether Taubes knew the titles: Adolf von Harnack, *Marcion. Der moderne Gläubige des 2. Jahrhunderts, der erste Reformator. Die Dorpater Preisschrift (1870),* and Harnack, [speech manuscript of the lecture] *Marcion: Der radikale Modernist des 2. Jahrhunderts* (1923), is relatively unimportant, because Taubes's modernity signifies that of the twentieth century, so a (once again) modernized Marcion(ism). (It is impossible that Taubes knew the texts themselves; both were first edited in 2003 by Friedemann Steck in Berlin/New York [de Gruyter].)

6. Ulrich Raulff, "Die Auserwählten," *Süddeutsche Zeitung* (8 Jan 2004), 11.

elitism of the first director of the Berlin Wissenschaftskolleg at the time, Peter Wapnewski, a discourse strongly influenced by Stefan George.[7] The "Conversation" quickly touched on fundamental issues, questioning as a whole the neo-Nietzscheanism still toxic today[8]: "I hope not to be unjust toward the 'constellation Nietzsche'—I say constellation, because it is more than a person, because the work of Nietzsche is burdened with implications that describe an era of history, and thus I place the constellation Nietzsche eye-to-eye with the constellation Paul. This is how Nietzsche himself sees it."

And indeed it was through Nietzsche that Taubes, the son of a rabbi, had first come across the Jewish arch-heretic Paul, perceiving him "as an opponent of Nietzsche." As Taubes put it, "Nietzsche wants to reverse the Christian values which Paul had built into the transvaluation of classical values. Nietzsche wants to *undo* Paul's transvaluation of the ancient values. This is the great horizon in which the Nietzsche-Paul controversy stands,"[9] precisely on the question: Elite or avant-garde?

When referring to 1 Cor 1:26, Taubes is certain: "Paul does not deny avant-garde, but he denies elite." As he glosses:

> "But see, dear brothers, your calling"—and "calling" means *élection*, elite—"not many wise according to the flesh, not many powerful, not many noble are called, but God has chosen the foolish things of the world to confound the wise; and God has chosen the weak things of the world to confound the things which are strong; and base things of the world, and things which are despised, has God chosen and things which are not, to bring to nothing the things that are, so that no flesh should glory in his presence.[10]

As Taubes further comments on this passage from Paul:

---

7. *Translators' note: Stefan George (1868–1933). For George's "afterlife" in post-war West Germany see also Ulrich Raulff, *Kreis ohne Meister* (Munich: Dt. Taschenbuch Verlag, 2009), and Richard Faber, "Aus Anlass von Ulrich Raulff's Buchpublikation 'Kreis ohne Meister. Stefan Georges Nachleben' (2010)," in *A propos: kulturwissenschaftliche Miszellen von und für Richard Faber*, edited by Christine Holste and Barbara von Reibnitz (Würzburg: Königshausen & Neumann, 2013), 150–154.

8. Even Peter Sloterdijk's much later eugenic fantasies of breeding humans are criticized in advance; cf. "J. Taubes im Gespräch mit W. von Rahden und N. Kapferer. Elite oder Avantgarde?," in *Tumult: Zeitschrift für Verkehrswissenschaft* 4 (1982), 75–76.

9. Ibid., 72, 74.

10. Ibid., 71.

So not the noble, the well-born, the wise according to the wisdom of this world are the ones elected, but precisely what is regarded as ignoble, is elected . . . But at first it is an avant-garde, a small community. Yet it is not determined by the measures valid in this world, but by measures that question the world as it is; in a way that Nietzsche was aware of and in a way that was expressed more brutally in a book by Alain de Benoist, this leader of the French Right . . . in which he speaks of the "Bolshevism of Christianity." This is not wrong. I mean, it is brutal, coarse, but in early Christianity there is a bit of Bolshevism. The "Bolshevist" bit is that it is addressed[11] "to all."[12]

Auerbach had similarly argued that the New Testament message "addresses everybody," using as his prime example the evangelist Mark's "report" on Peter's betrayal (M, 51). He highlighted its contrast with, for example, the Trimalchio–banquet of Petronius, which is not at all shy of vulgarisms.[13] At that time, Petronius's style was aimed precisely[14] at "the taste of a social-literary *élite* which views things from high up with coolness and indulgence," as Auerbach notes (M, 50). No wonder Taubes remembers Auerbach as explicitly and emphatically as he does in his 1968 essay "The Justification of Ugliness in Early Christian Tradition": "What Nietzsche only hinted at aphoristically and polemically, Erich Auerbach described with calm precision and enlightenment in his fragments toward a history of our sense of 'reality;'" by way of the sociology of religion Taubes emphasizes Auerbach's "fragments on a kind of *christological* history of literature."[15]

---

11. *Translators' note: *es geht an alle* refers to an act of addressing, as in a letter delivered to everybody. At the same time, *es geht alle an* means "it concerns everybody." Taubes's punctuation plays with both meanings.

12. Ibid., 71–72.

13. On the different characteristics of Petronian and New Testament 'vulgarisms,' see more extensively Erich Auerbach, *Literatursprache und Publikum in der lateinischen Spätantike und im Mittelalter* [Literary Language and Its Public in Late Latin Antiquity and in the Middle Ages] (Bern: Francke, 1958), 46–48.

14. *Translators' note: Faber creates an adverbial cluster here: *noch oder gerade*, "still or precisely," whereby "still" indicates the imminent waning of the elites.

15. Jacob Taubes, "Die Rechtfertigung des Häßlichen in urchristlicher Tradition," in *Die nicht mehr schönen Künste: Grenzphänomene des Ästhetischen* [The Not So Fine Arts Anymore: Borderline Phenomena of the Aesthetic], edited by Hans Robert Jauß (Munich: Fink, 1983), 169. Taubes may well have taken 'christological history of literature' from: Helmut Kuhn, 'Literaturgeschichte als Geschichtsphilosophie' [The History of Literature as Philosophy of History], *Philosophische Rundschau* 11 (1963), 248. But no doubt Taubes remodels Kuhn; the conservative-Catholic philosopher denies that

Humilitas qua Sublimitas

Here already, in the preceding sentence, Taubes has virtually melded Auerbach and Nietzsche by positing that Nietzsche had understood "the '*sermo humilis*' of Paul as a transvaluation of the religious, ethical, and aesthetic values of the ancient world."[16] Auerbach had done the same, as Taubes argues by citing the *"sermo humilis"* as a key concept. Here Taubes refers to the 1958 *Literary Language and Audience in Late Latin Antiquity and the Middle Ages*,[17] a collection of essays the author understood as a supplement to his major work *Mimesis*, published twelve years earlier. In what follows I will rely mainly on this book, which—at least around 1968—was Taubes's absolute favorite. One of my most lively and enduring memories of Taubes is when, back in the late sixties, he would come to talk about his most hated book, which he mimed trampling on—Arnold Gehlen's *Urmensch und Spätkultur* [Prehistoric Man and Later Culture]—to then talk about his most loved one, Auerbach's *Mimesis*, which he took into his arms to caressingly dance with it as if it were an eastern Jewish Torah scroll.[18]

Auerbach's "Christology" is orthodox, so that it is one only seemingly "pseudo-Christology"; whereas Taubes as a sympathizer of (Marcionite) "heresy" needs to have no qualms about Auerbach's 'christological history of literature.' In all likelihood he even felt indirectly confirmed by Kuhn's critique of Auerbach.

16. Taubes, "Die Rechtfertigung des Häßlichen," 169.

17. Auerbach *Literatursprache und Publikum in der lateinischen Spätantike und im Mittelalter*, 20ff.

18. I am not exaggerating, but leaving aside the anecdotal: Taubes regarded Auerbach's "Interpretation of a few sections" (M, 509), published under the title *Mimesis*, as a legitimate Bible commentary and—of course above all—as a masterly *interpretation* of the not illegitimate continuations of Bible writing in the more profane and in that regard also *more realistic* context of 'occidental' literature. (On the wider context of "Bibel und Literatur" [Bible and Literature] see, e.g., the volume of collected essays of the same name, edited by Jürgen Ebach and myself in Munich: Fink, 1995.)

Auerbach's approach to biblical literary scholarship (M, 315, 316 and 516) is of general cultural-historical and cultural-theoretical relevance, particularly in the German-speaking world, which was hellenocentric and even philhellenic (and romanophile) up until the 1970s. It is just as remarkable *today* that Auerbach did not fall into the other, 'pan-Judaist' extreme. Auerbach recognizes and acknowledges the whole 'méditerranée' as the origin of the 'occident' (M, 9, 13, 27, 76–77, 515; cf. also *Literatursprache und Publikum*, 66 and 259 and *Gesammelte Aufsätze*, 117); with this he anticipates a view that has gained acceptance in the latest *New Pauly* and hence in Classical philological quarters. (Cf. Hubert Cancik, "Altertum und Antikerezeption im Spiegel der Geschichte der Realencyclopädie (1839–1993)," in Cancik, *Antik, Modern: Beiträge zur römischen und deutschen Kulturgeschichte* (Stuttgart; Weimar: Metzler, 1998), 12–15. One should by no means overlook the fact that as a biblical scholar, which he is just as much as he is a classical philologist, Cancik makes different emphases than does Auerbach, specifically regarding the synoptics; cf. Cancik, "Die Gattung Evangelium. Das Evangelium des

Amongst other things, *Mimesis* has the advantage that Auerbach included in it one of his thematic essays, "*Sacrae scripturae sermo humilis*" (M, 74). Taubes drew my attention to this essay of 1941 when—in the early 1980s—I was working on the rhetoric of the anti-rhetorician Johann Peter Hebel, and on his own "*Sermo Humilis*."[19] Taubes generally defined the anti-rhetoric rooted in the Bible in a paradoxical way, when—emphasizing Auerbach—he formulated that the "Christian form of the sublime" is "the *sermo humilis*."[20] This short formula cuts Auerbach (and the matter in question) short, unless, like him, one begins with a "*new* 'sermo humilis'": a "low style to be used actually only for comedy and satire, yet which *now* reaches widely beyond its original sphere into the lowest and the highest, into the sublime and the eternal (M, 74)."[21]

As Auerbach emphasized, the narrative style of the Synoptic Gospels was a "*sermo piscatorius*," but nevertheless, or precisely for this reason, it

---

Markus im Rahmen der antiken Historiographie" [The Genre of Gospel: The Gospel of Mark in the Context of Ancient Historiography], *Humanistische Bildung* 4 (1981), 63–101, and Cancik, "Die Berufung des Johannes. Prophetische Tradition des Alten in der Geschichtsschreibung des Neuen Testaments" [Prophetic Tradition of the Old in the Writing of History in the New Testament], *Der Altsprachliche Unterricht* 25.2 (1982), 45–62.)

Regarding the inner-Jewish, it is noteworthy that Auerbach also acknowledges the New Testament and quite naturally integrates it into an all-biblical canon, even though he understands 'canon' as only socio-cultural; this is in complete contrast to e.g., Hermann Cohen and Gershom Sholem, but once again in accordance with Bloch, Taubes, and also Buber and Benjamin. (Cf. Ernst Bloch, *Atheismus im Christentum. Zur Religion des Exodus und des Reichs* [Frankfurt: 1968], as well as Jacob Taubes, "Walter Benjamin—ein moderner Marcionit?" [Walter Benjamin—A modern Marcionite?]; concerning Benjamin, see also Richard Faber, "Walter Benjamin und das 'Vater unser'—mehr als eine historisch-philologische Glosse" [Walter Benjamin and the Lord's Prayer—More than a Historical-Philological Commentary], *Zeitschrift für Religions- und Geistesgeschichte* 51 [1999] 70–74.)

19. Cf. Richard Faber, "Sermo humilis: Erzählung, Moral und Rhetorik Johann Peter Hebels," in *Spiegel und Gleichnis: Festschrift für Jacob Taubes*, edited by Norbert W. Bolz and W. Hübener (Würzburg: Königshausen & Neumann, 1983), 205–32, and Faber, "*Sagen lassen sich die Menschen nichts, aber erzählen lassen sie sich alles.*" [People won't let anyone have any say over them, but you can tell them anything.] *Über Grimm-Hebelsche Erzählung, Moral und Utopie in Benjaminscher Perspektive* (Würzburg: Königshausen & Neumann, 2002), especially chapters 1, 4, and 5. Already in 1948 Gerhard Hess identified Hebel as a very special "candidate" for Auerbach's *Mimesis* ("Zu Erich Auerbachs Geschichte des abendländischen Realismus," *Romanische Forschungen* 61 [1948] 192–93).

20. Taubes, "Die Rechtfertigung des Häßlichen," 169; Taubes relies on Auerbach, *Literatursprache und Publikum*, 22.

21. Cf. also Auerbach, *Literatursprache und Publikum*, 53.

was "much more effective than the highest rhetorical registers of the tragic work of art; and the most moving thing about these narratives was *the Passion*. That the King of kings was mocked, spat on, whipped, and nailed to the cross like a common criminal—this story, as soon as it governs the consciousness of humanity, completely destroys the aesthetics of stylistic separation; it generates a new *high* style, which does not at all spurn the quotidian, and which incorporates the sensorial-realistic, even the ugly, the unworthy, the physically base" (M, 74).

One should take heed: as a new low style develops, so does a new high one: as Auerbach emphasizes again and again, this new high one is a "mixed style" that makes all future realism (in a modern sense) possible in the first place.[22] But let us first consider the all-decisive question—asked from Paul to Taubes[23]—of the cross as such: the "*servile supplicium*," as Auerbach puts it in "The Justification of Ugliness in Early Christian Tradition."[24] In "Elite or Avant-garde?" Taubes (in the wake of Nietzsche) points out that Paul actually connects "the reversal of the image of elite" with the theology of the cross: "The promise . . . of the gospel . . . is that it goes out 'to all.' Therefore it is no coincidence at all that in one of the most remarkable texts [remarkable also in Auerbach's estimation[25]] of the Apostle Paul, where he speaks of 'God on the cross,' . . . Paul also speaks of the community and performs the reversal of the ancient concept of elite."[26]

Elsewhere Taubes argues: "For Paul, the social status of the community . . . , its status as a *pariah*, is the consequence and expression of the same divine weakness and foolishness of which the cross is the sign." Conversely,

> By writing to this community about its own place in the world, by writing about the election of the ignoble and those despised by the

---

22. This making-possible, like modern realism itself, is not my topic, but I venture to make a reference to: M, 34–35, 236–37, 246, 291, and 515.

23. On the gigantic role that Paul played for Taubes—up to the point of self-identification—informs us best, in all brevity: Christoph Schulte, "Paulus," in *Abendländische Eschatologie. Ad Jacob Taubes*, edited by Richard Faber et al. (Würzburg: Königshausen & Neumann, 2001), 93–103. (Of course Schulte also takes into account Taubes's "Paulus"-lectures included in his will and coedited by him, *Die Politische Theologie des Paulus* [Munich: Fink, 1993].) Of decisive importance here is that Taubes always includes Marcion when he mentions Paul. In fact, quite frequently "the Apostle" Paul is merely a *code name* for "the heretic" Marcion.

24. Taubes, "Die Rechtfertigung des Häßlichen," 184.

25. [Faber's insertion]

26. "J. Taubes im Gespräch mit W. v. Rahden und N. Kapferer," 71.

world, about [this election] which reverses and perverts the values of this world, Paul wants to demonstrate to them the paradox of the foolishness and weakness of God. Toward the end of the paragraph, Paul's message rises further. His reference to the reversing and perverting social position of the community becomes the 'metaphysical' judgment of the world in general. The social judgment changes into a metaphysical one. God has chosen what is not (*ta me onta*) to destroy what is (*ta onta*).[27]

Now this is *Marcionite* Paulinism in literary form. But I will insist—quite agreeing with Taubes—on the social: that Paul's teaching on the foolishness of the cross "flies in the face of *ancient noble convictions*."[28] And I will deepen the plebeian, even rebellious character of this teaching of the cross, before I come to speak of *political* Marcionism (especially Bloch's). But first one needs to return to Auerbach's sociology of *literary* religion: to his hypothesis that "the real core of the Christian teaching, Incarnation and Passion," was "fully incompatible with the principle of the *separation* of styles" (M, 73): "In ancient theory the high, sublime linguistic style was called *sermo gravis* or *sublimis*; the base one [was called] *remissus* or *humilis*; both had to remain strictly separate. In Christianity, in contrast, both are melded together from the beginning, especially in the Incarnation and Passion of Christ, in which *sublimitas* as well as *humilitas*, and both in excess, are realized and united" (M, 147).

To once again illustrate with Auerbach: "Christ did not appear as a hero or king, but as a human of the lowest social rank; his first disciples were fishermen and craftsmen, he moved around the quotidian environment of the small nation in Palestine, talked to tax collectors and prostitutes, to the poor and sick and to children; and every one of his actions and words was nevertheless of the highest and deepest dignity, more significant than whatever else usually took place; the style in which it was told was seen as rhetorically uncultured or raw; it was a *sermo piscatorius*, but still very moving" (M, 73–74).

---

27. Taubes, "Die Rechtfertigung des Häßlichen," 174; cf. also Taubes, "Die Entstehung des jüdischen Pariavolkes: Ideologiekritische Noten zu Max Webers 'Gesammelte Aufsätze zur Religionssoziologie,' vol. III, 'Das antike Judentum,'" in *Max Weber-Gedächtnisschrift der Ludwig-Maximilians-Universität München zum 100. Geburtstag 1964*, edited by Karl Engisch et al. (Berlin: Duncker and Humblot, 1966), 185–94.

28. Taubes, "Die Rechtfertigung des Häßlichen," 170.

Humilitas qua Sublimitas

Crucial to this approach, especially in the context of Marcionism that is to an extent anti-Jewish, is that "the sublime, the tragic, and the problematic"

> already takes shape *in the narratives of the Old Testament* . . . in the domestic and the quotidian: events like those between Cain and Abel; between Noah and his sons; between Abraham, Sarah, and Hagar; and between Rebekka, Jacob, and Esau are unimaginable in the Homeric style . . . In the stories of the Old Testament, the quietness of the daily goings-on in the house, in the field, and with the herds is constantly undermined by jealousy about the election and the promise of blessing, and entanglements develop that would be incomprehensible for the Homeric heroes. For them, what is needed is a concrete, clearly expressible reason for conflict and enmity to come about, and they take effect in free battles; whilst in the Biblical narratives the permanently smoldering jealousy as well as the link between the economic and the spiritual, between the fatherly blessing and the divine blessing, leads to a saturation of daily life with seeds of conflict and often to its poisoning. The sublime working of God intervenes so deeply into the quotidian that the two domains of the sublime and the quotidian are not only actually undivided, they are essentially indivisible. (M, 25–26)

It is thus clear that Auberbach had deeply thought about "Jewish-Christian literature" as a *unity*. (This does not contravene Taubes's reading of Auerbach as providing a "christological history of literature.") And by the way, he did so at the point where he comes to talk about the story of Peter's denial. Here one may recognize

> *at first glance* . . . that there can be no talk about a rule of stylistic separation. This certainly realistic scene, in terms of setting and characters, is at once analytically dense and deeply tragic. Peter is . . . in the highest and the lowest sense, in the most tragic sense, an image of the human. Of course there is no artistic intention in this mixture of stylistic spheres. Rather *from the beginning* it is founded in the character of Jewish-Christian Scripture, and was made [even] more obvious and glaring through the Incarnation of God in a man of the lowest social rank, his walking on earth amongst low, common people and conditions, and his, in worldly terms, disgraceful Passion; and of course, considering how widespread and influential these scriptures later became, it influenced most decisively the understanding of the tragic and the sublime. (M, 44)

Returning to the episode on Peter, Auerbach talks as a political sociologist, though he moves beyond class theory: Peter's entrance was, "like generally everything connected to Jesus' arrest, no more than a minor incident in the world-historical context of the Roman Empire, a local event without any significance which nobody except those closely involved takes notice of; just how enormous is it in comparison to the usual life of a fisherman from the Sea of Galilee, and what a tremendous swing of the pendulum (*Harnack* once used this very phrase when he talked about the Denial scene[29]) takes place in him!" (M, 45).

"Seen from outside," this is

> about a police operation and its consequences—it involves only ordinary people; in antiquity something like that could only be conceived as a farce or a comedy. But why does that not happen? Why does it arouse the most serious and greatest sympathy? Because it describes something that neither ancient poetry nor ancient history-writing has ever described before: the development of a [not purely] spiritual movement in the depth of ordinary people... which is at first almost fully confined to them, but then gradually... moves into the historical foreground—but already now, from the very beginning, this movement makes an open claim to immediately concern everyone.

And then, in a manner converging with Taubes and Bloch, Auerbach emphasizes: "For the authors of the New Testament, the current events unfolding in quotidian life are *revolutionary* world affairs. Later on they will be so for everyone" (M, 45–46[30]).

As we have heard, "everyone" is important, but the quotidian is "revolutionary" as well. This is the case as early as—or rather, again—with St. Francis and his own radical, "Spiritual" disciples.[31] Auerbach admire

---

29. In *Dante als Dichter der irdischen Welt* [Dante as a Poet of the Temporal World] (Leipzig: de Gruyter, 1928), 20, Auerbach refers explicitly to Adolf von Harnack, "Die Verklärungsgeschichte Jesu, der Bericht des Paulus I Kor. 15,3ff. und die beiden Christusvisionen des Petrus," in *Sitzber. Preuß. Ak. Wiss. Phil. Hist. Kl.* 1922. (Cf. also p. 25 n. 11, where Auerbach refers to a study of Augustine by Harnack.)

30. Cf. also E. Auerbach, *Dante als Dichter der irdischen Welt*, 19, where it says: Jesus "unleashed a movement in Jerusalem which *necessarily* could not remain *purely spiritual.*"

31. *Translators' note: Faber alludes to the Franciscan Spirituals and Joachimites mentioned next.

sFrancis as much as Bloch and Taubes greatly admire Joachim of Fiore (M, 163–64[32]):

> At the beginning of the 13th century a figure appears in Italy who in an exemplary way embodies the New Testament mixture of *sublimitas* and *humilitas*, of ecstatic, sublime unity with God and of humble, concrete ordinariness . . . ; it is Francis of Assisi. The essence of his person and the impact of his appearance are based on the will to radical and practical imitation of Christ; after the age of the martyrs had ended, faith had taken a mainly mystic-contemplative form. Francis gave it a [renewed] turn toward the practical, the quotidian, the public, and the folkloric. (M, 156[33])

I refrain here from delving into the Joachimite Franciscan Spirituals, Hussites, Thomas Münzer, etc.; and I mention only Rabelais, whom Auerbach saw within the Franciscan tradition (M, 163[34]). Instead, together with Auerbach I jump across centuries into the *modern*-proletarian milieu as it was described especially by Émile Zola.

Especially in the case of *Germinal*, published in 1888, Auerbach without a doubt again diagnoses "a mixture of humble and sublime in which, for the sake of content, the latter is dominant": it is a "great historical tragedy" (M, 477[35]). And in terms of reception history he explains: "What filled

---

32. Concerning Bloch, I refer to his "Zur Originalgeschichte des Dritten Reiches" [On the Original History of the Third Reich] in: Ernst Bloch, *Erbschaft dieser Zeit* [Inheritance of Our Time] (Frankfurt: Suhrkamp, 1973), 126–52. Besides the chapters on Joachim of Fiore in Taubes's *Abendländische Eschatologie* [Occidental Eschatology] (Munich: Matthes und Seitz, 1991, 77ff., 90f., and 98ff.), see his "Die Intellektuellen und die Universität," in: Taubes, *Vom Kult zur Kultur. Bausteine zu einer Kritik der historischen Vernunft* [From Cult to Culture: Building Blocks for a Critique of Historical Reason] (Munich: Fink, 1996), 319ff. Among new works on Joachim is to be mentioned that of Matthias Riedl, *Joachim von Fiore. Denker der vollendeten Menschheit* [Joachim of Fiore: Thinker of the Perfected Humanity] (Würzburg: Königshausen & Neumann, 2004). Riedl (harshly) criticizes Bloch and Taubes on details, but on essential points also agrees with them; cf. above all 235–41, 245, 251, 257, 260–70, 283–84, 291, 294–97, 307–8, 321, 330, 337–41.

33. Cf. also Auerbach, *Gesammelte Aufsätze zur romanischen Philologie*, 33ff. and 43ff.

34. Cf. also Jürgen Link and Ursula Link-Heer, who relativize Auerbach: "Karwoche oder Karneval? Auerbach und Bachtin über literarische Realistik," in *Poetologische Umbrüche. Romanistische Studien zu Ehren von Ulrich Schulz-Buschhaus*, edited by Werner Helmich et al. (Munich: Fink, 2002), 405–27.

35. Conversely and congruently it says in the *Dante*-book of 1928: "The depth and extent of *naturalism* in the story of Christ is unique." One page later he talks about "the mimetic potential of the story of Christ" as such (22–23). This formulation leaves no

[Zola's opponents] with agitation 'was . . . the fact that Zola by no means presented his art as one of "low style" or as comical; almost each one of his lines reveals that everything is meant completely seriously and morally; that the whole thing is certainly not amusement or an artistic game, but the true image of contemporary society as he, Zola, saw it; and as he asked the audience in these works to see it as well'" (M, 474).

As Harnack had already done in 1920, Auerbach finally comes to talk of "*Russian* realism," despite or precisely because of the observation "that it is grounded in a Christian Old-Patriarchal image of the creaturely dignity of each and every human being, no matter of which estate or in which situation; hence that in its foundations it is more closely related to ancient Christian tradition than to modern West European realism" (M, 484)—even more so, one could say in view of Auerbach's own Zola-characteristics. As he does with the story of Peter in the Gospel of Mark, Auerbach in particular recalls the extremely wide (and *Harnackian*) "swing of the pendulum" in the essence, actions, thoughts, and feelings of the characters in Dostoyevski, Tolstoy, and "the other" Russians (M, 485–86), but also the revolutionary characters *before* and alongside them. They, "the reformers, the indignant, and the conspirators, which appear *in large numbers*," were still "closely bound up with the Christian Old Patriarchal world, from which they could only tear themselves away with torturous violence" (M, 484).

In any event, at the end of the chapter dedicated to, amongst others, Zola, Tolstoy, and "the other Russians," Auerbach is convinced: ". . . if, since the last decade before the First World War, the moral crisis had been deepening in many places, including in realist literature, and something like an intimation of the imminent catastrophes could be felt, then the influence of the Russian realists *substantially* contributed to this" (M, 487[36]).

The young Bloch in *The Spirit of Utopia* and Harnack two years later in *The Gospel of the Alien God* thought no differently, only that they—with Taubes's much later concept—saw modern Marcionism where Auerbach, almost confusingly, saw the heritage of Christian Old Patriarchalism at work. Taubes refers in 1984 to Bloch's greatest teacher Max Weber, who—as

---

doubt about the *Dante*-book's fundamental importance for the *Mimesis*-book.

36. Concerning the imminent catastrophes which have by now long occurred, one should by all means associate here the sentence with which Auerbach's "Epilegomena to *Mimesis*" ends: "*Mimesis* quite consciously is a book written by a particular person, in a particular situation, at the beginning of the 1940s" (*Romanische Forschungen* 65 (1953), 18)—at the height of the "catastrophes."

Edith Hanke has shown[37]—was powerfully fascinated and even awed by Tolstoy (as he was by Nietzsche[38]):

> Weber traced the origins of the rational lifestyle of the capitalist epoch from the spirit of the Protestant-inner-worldly asceticism up to the dialectical turning-point, that is, up to the denial of any asceticism in the late-capitalist society of affluence: "As asceticism was transferred out of the monks' cubicles into professional life and began to govern inner-worldly morality, it helped build the mighty cosmos of the modern economy which today governs the lifestyle of all with overwhelming force." As Christian election becomes "inner-worldly" in the Protestant ethos (i.e., "practical"), "doom" turns our modern world into a "steel-hard shell." But what is it like living in a "steel-hard shell?" "Nobody knows yet who will live in that shell in the future and whether at the end of this development there will be wholly new prophets or just mechanized fossils." Max Weber's prognosis at the end of his study of capitalism has become reality since the end of the First World War, when the spiritual march of progress parading through science and technology came to a halt. The "steel-hard shell" is called "doom" by Max Weber with noble intentions—a Gnostic hieroglyph, which can be deciphered in the different modes of attempted exodus out of the steel-hard shell.[39]

As Taubes is convinced, "The Gnostic hieroglyph of that epoch after the First World War up until the inheritance of that epoch, and the controversy about that inheritance, can be made clear" above all "in the argument about *Marcion*." And: "Marcion marks the *parting* of the ways."[40] Taubes probably also thought of Carl Schmitt and Hans Blumenberg, with whose controversial relationship to Marcion I have dealt elsewhere.[41]

---

37. Cf. Edith Hanke, *Prophet des Unmodernen: Leo N. Tolstoi als Kulturkritiker in der deutschen Diskussion der Jahrhundertwende* (Tübingen: Niemeyer, 1993), esp. Part 2, Chapter III, 168–208.

38. Concerning the great proximity between Weber and Nietzsche in Taubes's view, cf. Andreas Urs Sommer, "'Pathos der Revolution' im 'stahlharten Gehäuse' des 'Verhängnisses.' Marginalien zum Thema 'Max Weber bei Jacob Taubes,'" in *Abendländische Eschatologie*, edited by Faber et al., 365–71.

39. Cf. Jacob Taubes, "Das stählerne Gehäuse und der Exodus daraus oder ein Streit um Marcion, einst und heute," in *Gnosis und Politik*, edited by Jacob Taubes (Munich: Fink, 1984), 10.

40. Ibid., 11.

41. Cf. Richard Faber, *Der Prometheus-Komplex: Zur Kritik der Politotheologie Eric Voegelins und Hans Blumenbergs* (Würzburg: Königshausen & Neumann, 1984), Part B.;

Political Demonology

What follows is about *Bloch*, who understands his œuvre as a testimony to "*revolutionary* Gnosis"—"in the spirit of the arch-heretic Marcion, this most important interpreter of the Apostle Paul, whose 'Gospel of the alien God' like a revolutionary smashes the tablets of values so much that all church-Christians . . . would cross themselves before Marcion's teaching if only they knew about him."[42] Up to this point I have considered Taubes; from now on I will directly follow Bloch (whom Taubes, following the early Walter Benjamin, *de*interprets on a decisive point[43]).

Bloch's Marcion argues that Paul, unlike he himself, did not "contradict Yahweh as the creator of the world, but instead as the *law-giver*. Paul [first] put that hiatus between 'law' and 'gospel,' also between the 'morality of the law' and 'freedom,' 'justice' and 'grace,' so that Jesus should at least become unique" (A, 239[44]). But even beyond this Marcionite resolution of the Pauline *dialectics* of law and gospel, Marcion extends the dualism between the two, which in fact he postulated first, to the creator and the redeemer god, or lets their duality, as the earlier and more fundamental duality, precede or rather found the dialectic. Either way the law is in effect assigned to the world's creator, who then tyrannically rules over the world, and the gospel to the "alien god" Jesus, who is the god of consolation.[45] This divine duality "sharpens"—as Bloch expresses himself—the antithesis between law and gospel that is not correctly Pauline in any case "to the point of *irreconcilability* and hence also the radical *novum*," which is how Marcion distinguishes the Gospel from the Old Testament (A, 239).

Intriguingly he synonymizes the radical nature of the gospel's novelty with "foreignness" and also calls the redeeming god of the gospel "alien." This god "does not call us home from foreign lands where we have gotten lost, but from the horrific home to which we belong, into a blessed foreign land."[46] This is not Bloch's, but rather the formulation of the Marcion-scholar Harnack. But he does so in exactly the same sense as Bloch (perhaps inspired by him). As late as in his *Atheism*, for instance, Bloch speaks of

---

below as Excursus I.

42. Taubes, "Walter Benjamin—ein moderner Marcionit?," 139.

43. Cf. ibid.

44. "A" here and in the following stands for: Ernst Bloch, *Atheismus im Christentum: Zur Religion des Exodus und des Reichs* [Atheism in Christianity: The Religion of the Exodus and the Kingdom] (Frankfurt: Suhrkamp, 1968).

45. Cf. Carsten Colpe, "'Das eschatologische Widerlager der Politik.' Zu Jacob Taubes's Gnosisbild," in *Abendländische Eschatologie*, edited by Faber et al., 124.

46. Harnack, *Marcion*, 225.

"something which shines into everyone's childhood, but where no one has ever been: home" (A, 294)—as he already had done in the *Principle of Hope*, where he seems to be "orchestrating"[47] Harnack.

Certainly a problem for Bloch's understanding of Marcion is this extreme ascetic's escape from the world, even enmity towards it. The problem is that the message of this most extreme theologian of the exodus, because he leads out of *all* worldliness, is that it is, in Bloch's understanding, "itself dark."

> For it not only leads out of captivity, like the great archetype of the exodus in the Old Testament excluded by Marcion, but out of the flesh and out of every temporality, and not into a better one. This purely pneumatic, purely *logos*–mythical farewell to the world in its asceticism sees no land before itself, one where—at least comparatively—milk and honey flow. And according to this purely pneumatic docetism of the Marcionites it became even less true that Christ had risen in flesh. Indeed the true Christ was not even born in flesh for them; thus flawed, the message of the wholly new, wholly alien god according to Marcion could not have given an impulse of such purity. Meanwhile, also here, also in this abstract asceticism so often trivialized, also with this flipside of a total orientation towards the alien in Marcion's god, there is no evidence of a turn away from the human being in this world.

Bloch is convinced; "on the contrary: what was envisioned was an even more complete turn toward the human. Toward his own, specifically designated transcendence into the foreignness of a home that is singularly identical with him" (A, 240).

Well, this is already a further developed, a "modern,"[48] a *Blochian* Marcion we are introduced to here. But this atheist philosopher, or rather this philosophical atheist, *always* thinks further than, but also beyond, both humanism and the Enlightenment. *In doing so* he recurs, in order to transcend the historical Enlightenment, to the pre-Enlightened, the religious, though always the potentially utopian. Bloch is always concerned with what will be better in the future; in that regard, one can and even should by all means polemicize against "*the existing* world," the more so when it is understood—in an apocalyptic rather than Marcionite way—as "this aeon," and when this aeon is juxtaposed with another, better one in the

---

47. Cf. Taubes, "Das stählerne Gehäuse und der Exodus daraus," 11.
48. Once again I refer to Taubes, "Walter Benjamin—ein moderner Marcionit?"

sense of—irony of ironies—"new *world*." There is no question that "the old one" has gone "awry"; if that were not the case, "there would be no need for a messiah" (A, 173). But there is a need for one, even if it is a fully human, indeed collective messiah: in every sense *human-some* (A, 183), and in that regard of course also containing *world*, and world-*capable*.

There is a need for rebels and revolutionaries who can and should learn from the heretics spearheaded by Marcion. Speaking only in a historical sense, Harnack—a right-wing rather than left-wing liberal—stated what I repeat here: that Tolstoy is

> a Marcionite Christian through and through. The directly religious passages we have from Marcion could well have been written by him, and conversely Marcion would have recognized himself in Tolstoy's "miserable and despised," in his reading of the Sermon on the Mount . . . and in his zeal against common Christendom. On the other hand, Gorky's moving play *The Lower Depths* can be understood as a Marcionite play as well; "The Stranger" who appears here is the Marcionite Christ, and his "Lower Depths" are the world.[49]

No doubt what is meant is the miserable *social* world.

In Bloch's view it should be "blown up" by way of revolution (A, 148); here he is commemorating Marcion and certainly also thinking *normatively*. With reference to abrupt, immediate novelty he writes: "Jesus' birth . . . took place in the year zero." And:

> Interpreted in a *Marcionite* way, the year zero . . . is completely different from the starting points for counting within history, which hence merely occur, such as the Roman *ab urbe condita*. Paradoxically one could only recall the new beginning of the Jacobins' year zero, "likewise" intended to be total; its tearing away from the whole "Old Testament" of history as purely the fraud of dukes and clerics. But in this incomparably different, that is, religious topos, Marcion also rejects, with full *primeurs*, any possible historical mediation before his novum. (A, 241–42)

One should take note of how Bloch almost didactically draws an analogy, which is our sole concern here: he explicitly compares the "incomparably" different only in view of *the same* understanding of time as a radical break, the sudden and strict separation of the old and the new. Precisely with that aim, he can then *analogically* call the year of Jesus'

---

49. Harnack, *Marcion*, 232.

birth "year zero" (following the example of the French Revolution) and the *ancien régime* (following the example of the "Old Covenant") "Old Testament." In a kind of circular argument, this is about the immanentization of Jewish-Christian, specifically Marcionite *topoi* after they have already been re-interpreted or rather "charged" with immanent and *social-revolutionary* meaning.

This kind of Christianity in revolutionary atheism, or rather this kind of atheism in revolutionary Christianity, is not for everyone—today less so than ever. That neither of the two—at least historically—is a chimera, one can already learn from Max Weber, Bloch's teacher as well as his most decisive opponent. I would like to refer to Philippe Despoix's magisterial essay "Poetic Prophecy and Polytheistic Narration," in which—along with St. Paul, the synoptics, and Tolstoy—Nietzsche, Auerbach, and Taubes play a prominent role.

Despoix's work on Max Weber's implicit definition of the literary medium ends with the conviction: "Certainly the atheist Weber thought that the highest form of sociology is to say what the divine is in any given society." Despoix here presumes a widely held belief, possibly also Auerbach's own, that "'literary' media . . . bear the most visible traces of 'the divine.'"[50] This idea is connected to a complementary one, which Auerbach *makes plausible*: that it is above all in "the occident" that "divine" texts give us an idea of "literary" media; put in a Nietzschean way, that they give us an idea about their "genealogy." All scholars that I mention and discuss, no matter which "discipline" they belong to, more or less connect the sociology of literature with the sociology of religion and so prove the heuristic fertility—if not necessity—of this connection: of what in 1989 I called with a neologism "the politology of religious literature."[51]

And what about Karlheinz Barck, who is to be honored here via Auerbach? Drawing on Auerbach, Barck also engaged with Taubes's theorem of "modern Marcionism," and intervened specifically in the discussion provoked by Taubes, that philosopher of religion, about: "*surrealism* and Gnosis" instead of *realism*. I refer to my friend "Carlo" Barck's contribution to the volume *Abendländische Eschatologie: Ad Jacob Taubes*, which

50. Philippe Despoix, "Dichterische Prophetie und polytheistisches Erzählen. Zu Max Webers impliziter Bestimmung des literarischen Mediums," in *Kunst und Religion. Studien zur Kultursoziologie und Kulturgeschichte*, edited by Richard Faber and Volker Krech (Würzburg: Königshausen & Neumann, 1999), 97.

51. [*Religionsliteraturpolitologie.*] Cf. Faber, *Erbschaft jener Zeit. Zu Ernst Bloch und Hermann Broch* (Würzburg: Königshausen & Neumann, 1989), 9.

I edited.[52] Finally, I content myself with the following note: in 1929 Bloch had *sympathetically* talked about the "Thinking Surrealisms" of Walter Benjamin's "One-Way Street."[53] With this he signified a corpus of texts that no doubt also contains "modern Marcionisms"—not in Taubes's, but in Bloch's sense.[54] (In particular I'm thinking of texts such as "Fire Alarm."[55])

2. AUERBACH AND ADORNO

The last, if not the first, question to be answered is: "Where is the 'modern Marcionism' in Auerbach, the very one to be honored here?" But is this question not reduced to absurdity by the question with which Auerbach closed his 1933 essay "Romanticism and Realism": " . . . how could the order and truth of what is real possibly be imagined without seeing God in it?" One has to put this question in context:

> Once, long before the Romantic era, a tragic realism already existed, which regarded our disordered world as the true reality, so that it was ordered. I mean the tragic realism of the Middle Ages and its source, the story of Christ. In contrast to antiquity, it is the most radical destruction of the principle of stylistic separation, and altogether the most radical realization of tragic realism; it developed out of God's giving himself to worldly reality. The reality of our world today has changed so much that simply reaching back would make no sense. But *how could the order and truth of what is real possibly be imagined without seeing God in it?*[56]

No doubt, merely reaching back to the Middle Ages or (early) Christian antiquity and its characteristic *incarnational* faith in God seems to "make no sense" to Auerbach. But then how could the *thought* of God

---

52. Karlheinz Barck, "Jacob Taubes und der Surrealismus," in *Abendländische Eschatologie*, edited by Faber et al., 311–18.

53. Ernst Bloch, *Erbschaft dieser Zeit* (Frankfurt: Suhrkamp 1973), 367ff.

54. One should never forget the dedication of this book: "This street is called ASYA-LACIS-STREET after the [militant Marxist, R.F.] engineer who broke it open in the author" (Walter Benjamin, *Einbahnstraße* [Frankfurt: Suhrkamp, 1969] 5) Moreover, by now one should emphatically refer to Erdmut Wizisla, *Benjamin und Brecht. Die Geschichte einer Freundschaft* (Frankfurt: Suhrkamp, 2004).

55. Cf. Benjamin, *Einbahnstraße*, 76–77; regarding the later Benjamin, one should above all refer to the XV. of his theses "On the Concept of History."

56. Erich Auerbach, "Romantik und Realismus," *Neue Jahrbücher für Wissenschaft und Jugendbildung* 9 (1933), 153; emphasis added.

which he held in principle be any other than the thought of an alien "God," one who is yet to come, redeeming or precisely *newly* creating and ordering? We may additionally look at his essay "Baudelaire's *Fleurs du Mal* and the Sublime" (1951), which is mentioned neither by Barck nor by Taubes. It explicitly declares this emphatically modern lyric poet to be the bridge-builder between realism and surrealism, despite the fact that he is imputed to display a "mixed level of styles," and that here, Russian realism is also recalled: "The human figure appearing in them [the *Fleurs du Mal*] is as important as is the figure of Ivan Karamasov, whether it be for the destruction or the transformation of the European tradition."[57]

Even Harnack is indirectly mentioned again when Auerbach talks about the enormous "swing of the pendulum," specifically of the *Fleurs du Mal*.[58] After all, several pages earlier it reads:

- the only time when Christ appears in the text, he is "played off against God";[59]
- Baudelaire's hope was not "for redemption by God's grace, but the 'absolute Elsewhere.'"

    And—irony of ironies—this hope for a "way out" out of the "dungeon" of the world was "bitterly" hope*less*. Auerbach consistently calls the *Fleurs du Mal* "a work of despair."[60]

I shall explain this much more Adornian than Blochian Marcionism by recurring to Baudelaire's, Adorno's, and others' work on the myth of "Tasso."[61] The mature Goethe passed this judgment on *Lord Byron*: "He was so very dark about himself. He always passionately lived a life of leisure, and never knew or considered what he was doing. Taking the liberty to do everything, but never approving of anything in others, he was bound to fall out with himself and instigate the world against himself. . . . Everywhere was too narrow for him, and in the most uninhibited personal freedom he felt anxious. The world was like a prison to him."[62]

---

57. Erich Auerbach, *Gesammelte Aufsätze*, 277–79 and 290.

58. Ibid., 289.

59. Ibid., 285.

60. Ibid., 285–88.

61. More extensively: Richard Faber, *Der Tasso-Mythos. Eine Goethe-Kritik* [The Myth of Tasso: A Critique of Goethe] (Würzburg: Königshausen & Neumann, 1999); what follows is largely identical with 374–80 of that book.

62. Johann Peter Eckermann, *Gespräche mit Goethe in den letzten Jahren seines*

Political Demonology

These remarks may appear as a "counter-song to Alfonso's characterization of Tasso" in Goethe's *Tasso*;[63] I list the well-known keywords: darkness about oneself, passion, the liberty to do everything, and "instigating the world against oneself." *Definitive* doom and especially the prison *of the world* is only the case in Byron's *Tasso* and—besides Byron himself—the *Tasso* of Delacroix and Baudelaire, inspired by Byron. In "The Lament of Tasso," as its title suggests, the Englishman was the first to make the prison the (only) setting of Tasso's *tragedy*.

The "Lament" begins with the display of the mental, spiritual, and physical decay wrought by many years of life in a dark, musty prison cell with scarce, bland food. It evokes the screams of the tormented and tortured insane, crammed together in the rooms above Tasso. We are reminded of Tasso's passionate and doomed love for Eleonora d'Este. Yet in their repetition and increasing intensity Tasso's lamentations are more than a description of *his* conditions. The dungeon becomes the image for the narrowness of existence, the world as a whole.[64]

With all this, Byron inspired Baudelaire (via Delacroix), but not with his own aesthetic hope for the *power* of beauty and poetry. Throughout, "The Lament of Tasso" is accompanied by a hymn to poetic beauty, so that melancholy is sublated into aesthetic transcendence. In both the idea and affect of melancholy Byron remains congruent with Baudelaire. Passion and melancholy, despair and rebellion are "Byronesque" themes also characteristic of the *Fleurs du Mal*. But hope is excluded from them. Poetry as a way of *rescue*, of *overcoming* melancholy, is no longer mentioned in Baudelaire:[65]

> The poet in prison, unkempt and sick,
> With convulsed foot crushes a manuscript,
> His eyes seize, with terror shot through,
> The stairs for his soul, descent to vertigo.
>
> The frenzied laughter filling the prison
> To the Strange and Absurd invite his reason;
> Doubt surrounds him, and Fear is mocking,
> Hideous, multiform, into circles they lock him.

Lebens, 1823-1832. vol. 1, Berlin (without year), 150.

63. Cf. Maria Moog-Grünwald, "Tassos Leid. Zum Ursprung moderner Dichtung" [The Pains of Tasso. On the Origin of Modern Poetry], *Arcadia* 21 (1986), 113–28, 117.

64. Cf. ibid., 119.

65. Cf. ibid., 123.

Humilitas qua Sublimitas

> This spirit trapped in an unhealthy hole
> These grimaces, cries, the swarm of spectres
> Whirling, a swirling pack behind his ear,
>
> This dreamer, in his quarters roused by horror,
> Now here is your image, O spirit entangled,
> By Reality's walls suffocated and mangled.[66]

Baudelaire's Tasso is definitively suffocated, *and* he is so without any *poetic* transcendence, however sublimated it may be. From the very beginning his defense against what is threatening him is futile; his paralysis rushes *unstoppably* towards death. The threat is the same *reality* to which Baudelaire the author is also subject; despite all stylization,[67] his "Tasso in prison" is a *self*-portrait: Baudelaire's *"Mon cœur mis à nu"* is a self-portrait and hence explicitly a heart *exposing* itself, as Goethe's friend Carl Friedrich Zelter condemned it in the example of Beethoven & Co.[68] Nevertheless, one could at first hold the opinion that Baudelaire's expressionism merely pushes to the extreme what can *in nuce* be found already in Goethe's *Tasso*, especially in the verses "Though in their mortal anguish men are dumb / To me a God hath given to tell my grief":[69]

> In gloomy vaults of inscrutable sadness,
> Where hostile Fate already cast me,
> Where no beam ever enters, bright and rosy,
> Where I'm alone with Night, a sullen hostess,
>
> I'm like a painter; the mocking God—alas! to art
> Condemns me, to brush-strokes into darkness;
> Where, a cook of appetites macabre,

---

66. *Translators' own version of Charles Baudelaire, *Sur Le Tasse en prison d'Eugène Delacroix*, in *Les Fleurs du Mal* (1868); Faber cites Baudelaire, *Die Blumen des Bösen*, trans. by Therese Robinson, edited by Fr. Blei (Dreieich: Melzer, 1981), 162.

67. Tobias Bube kindly directed me to the section in *Mimesis* where Auerbach connects Baudelaire with the Goncourts (M, 464), though without identifying Baudelaire with their aestheticism of the "ugly, repulsive, and morbid." On decisive matters Baudelaire is closer to Zola than to the Goncourts. With this he also demonstrates that he is an heir of a Romanticism that never simply resisted Realism. (I refer again to Auerbach's 1933 essay "Romantik und Realismus.")

68. Goethe-Zelter, *Briefwechsel* (Zürich: Artemis Verlag, 1987), 64–65.

69. *Translators' note: "*Und wenn der Mensch in seiner Qual verstummt/Gab mir ein Gott zu sagen wie ich leide*" (*Tasso* V.5). English in: Johann Wolfgang von Goethe, *Torquato Tasso*, transl. *Goethe's Works*, vol. 3 (Philadelphia: G. Barrie, 1885). Faber cites: Johann Wolfgang von Goethe, *Sämtliche Werke*. Artemis Gedenkausgabe. *dtv–Dünndruck* (Munich, 1977), vol. 6, 313.

Political Demonology

I boil and eat my heart.[70]

But after these stanzas, arguing that Goethe's *Tasso* is pushed to the extreme would be much too straightforward: the person lamenting here is "doomed" to paint by a "god" inclined to malicious jokes. The god has turned the painting poet into a cannibal of himself: he boils and ingests his own heart.

It is well known that Baudelaire was convinced hell was "here";[71] this is consistent only for someone who is a Marcionite such as himself, one who thought that *the world* was a prison created by an *evil* creator. Regarding the political aspect of Baudelaire's gnosis, I will confine myself to the well-known works of the "modern Marcionite" Benjamin,[72] and now turn to *Adorno*. Adorno was equally interested in Marcion's "denunciation of the creator god."[73] "If at the centre of the *Meditations on Metaphysics* stands the question 'Can one live after Auschwitz?' (GS 6, p. 355)," remarked Adorno's editor Rolf Tiedemann on this passage from a letter, "then the connection with Marcion's accusation of the malicious god is obvious enough."[74]

Auschwitz and its consequences: this is also Auerbach's, Bloch's, and Taubes's topic, whether explicitly or implicitly.[75] However, Adorno was *fundamentally* steeped in it: "The need to give suffering a voice is the condition of all truth. For suffering is an objectivity burdening the subject; what the subject experiences as its most intensely subjective, its *expression*, is objectively mediated." This is certainly the case; but for the sake of reference to *Tasso*, we will emphasize the subjective side, citing Adorno's formulation of the "expressive *urge* of the subject." It is followed by the "freedom of

70. Charles Baudelaire, "Un Fantôme. I. Les Ténèbres," in *Les Fleurs du Mal* (1868); *Die Blumen des Bösen*, 60.

71. Cf. Walter Benjamin, *Illuminationen: Ausgewählte Schriften*, 2nd ed. (Frankfurt: Suhrkamp, 1969), 260.

72. Additionally, see Wolfgang Fietkau, *Schwanengesang auf 1848. Ein Rendezvous am Louvre: Baudelaire, Marx, Proudhon und Victor Hugo* (Reinbek bei Hamburg: Rowohlt, 1978).

73. Theodor W. Adorno, *Metaphysik Begriff und Probleme* (1965), edited by Rolf Tiedemann, (Frankfurt: Suhrkamp, 1998), 235.

74. Ibid.

75. Concerning Auerbach, I would like to recall once again his "Epilegomena zu Mimesis," and additionally Earl Jeffrey Richards, "Erich Auerbach's *Mimesis* as a Meditation on the Shoa," *German Politics and Society XIX*, 59 (Summer 2001), 62–91. Concerning Bloch, I refer to *Atheism in Christianity*, 319ff., and in the case of Taubes once again Christoph Schulte's contribution to the collection *Abendländische Eschatologie* is to be consulted.

philosophy," which now consists no more than in "helping it express its very lack of freedom."

Could one say, as Hans Kudzus supposed, that "the ability to think the disaster" was for Adorno "the most subtle joy of thinking"?[76] No doubt Adorno has posed the rhetorical question: "Is being capable of suffering not the only guarantor of happiness?" Yet he immediately added that "this can be no maxim."[77] Nevertheless, the reformulation of suffering and the restitution of the capacity to suffer is the force of resistance that Adorno's *Critical Theory* in general, and his *Aesthetic Theory* in particular, are meant to convey. The reason: "The potential of a positive is contained in the negation of the negation, that is, in itself a state of negativity, of suffering."[78] Art as much as philosophy—the two repeatedly go together for Adorno[79]—is defined as the "awareness of *sorrow*." As long as there is such an awareness, neither philosophy nor art could come to an end, since suffering finds its voice only in them: "the consolation that does not betray [suffering] right away." The greatest artists of the epoch had abided by this principle: "The uncompromising radicalism of their works, and especially the moments chided as formalistic, gives them this terrible force that is lacking in helpless poems dedicated to the victims."[80]

Adorno argues like no other in this section surrounding his dictum: "to write poetry after Auschwitz would be barbaric."[81] This is by no means forgotten when I now turn to music: Thomas Mann's novel *Dr. Faustus* about a *composer*, partly inspired by Adorno—primarily for the sake of the demand for consolation that does *not* betray the suffering. The recurrence to "Serenus Zeitblom's" final interpretation of "Doctor Faust's Lament" allows us to comprehend what has become of the musical lament beyond Goethe/Zelter and Beethoven[82]—what had to, or rather *should* become of it in Adorno's and Thomas Mann's view.

---

76. Hans Kudszus, "Die Kunst versöhnt mit der Welt," in Über Theodor W. Adorno (Frankfurt: 1969), 34.

77. Theodor W. Adorno, *Vorlesungen zur Ästhetik 1967-1968* (Zürich: H. Mayer Nachfahren, 1973), XI, or rather, 20.

78. Ibid., 20.

79. Cf. also Adorno, *Metaphysik*, 218.

80. Theodor W. Adorno, *Noten zur Literatur III* (Frankfurt: Suhrkamp, 1969), 125–26.

81. Ibid.; cf. also Adorno, *Metaphysik*, 172–74.

82. Cf. Faber, *Der Tasso-Mythos*, 373–74.

Political Demonology

The orchestral final movement of Adrian Leverkühn's *testamentary* lament sounds

> like God lamenting the loss of his world, like the creator's woeful "I did not want it" . . . Here, towards the end, the most extreme pitches of mourning are reached, despair has become an expression, and . . . it would be to damage the uncompromising nature of the work, its incurable pain, if one were to say: up until the last note there is another consolation but the expression itself, becoming audible—the consolation that the creature is given a voice for its suffering at all. No, until the end, this musical poem does not allow for any consolation, reconciliation, transfiguration. But what if the artistic paradox, that expression—expression as lament—is born out of a total construction, was akin to the religious paradox: that in the deepest hopelessness lies the seed of hope, if only as the most tender question? It would be hope beyond hope, the transcendence of despair—not its betrayal, but the miracle beyond belief. Just listen to the end, listen to it with me: one group of instruments after the other falls silent, and what remains is the high G of a cello, the last word, the last lingering note, slowly fading away in *pianissimo-fermata*. And then there is nothing—silence and night. But the note remains vibrating in the silence, the note that is no more, that only the soul can hear, the dying fall of lament, it is this no more; it changes its meaning, and stands like a light in the dark.[83]

A lot in this passage is Adornian: the Marcionite beginning, the generally negative theological approach, and finally the "hope against all hope."[84] Above all, this last lays the trace back to Goethe, though the Goethe *critically* rescued by Benjamin. Zeitblom's final words—"the note remains vibrating in the silence . . . and stands like a light in the dark"—almost reads like a Goethe quote from Benjamin's essay "Elective Affinities," which was central for him: "Like a star falling from the sky, hope shot across their heads." The "Elective Affinities" essay ropes it in *against* Goethe, and concludes: "Hope is only given to us for the hopeless' sake."[85] With Zeitblom's final sentence in mind, one should cite the following from Adorno: "As long as the world is what it is, all images of reconciliation, peace, and quiet resemble the im-

---

83. Thomas Mann, *Doktor Faustus* (Frankfurt: S. Fischer, 1967), 650–51.

84. Cf. also Thomas Macho, "Hermeneutik der Tränen. Notizen zu Hans Blumenberg's 'Matthäuspassion,'" *Neue Rundschau* 109 (1998), 61–77, especially 66.

85. Walter Benjamin, "Goethes Wahlverwandschaften," in *Gesammelte Schriften*, vol. 1 (Frankfurt: Suhrkamp, 1974), 201.

age of death. The refuge of hope would be the minute difference between Nothing and the one finding rest, a no-man's-land between the boundaries of Being and Nothing."[86]

This passage from Adorno may be found in the following context:

> [Samuel] Beckett alone reacted appropriately to the concentration camps—which he never mentions, as if the prohibition against idolatry hung over it. Whatever is, may it be as the concentration camp was. Once he talks about a lifelong death sentence. The only hope is that nothing would exist any longer. But he dismisses even that. From this fissure of inconsistency the imagery of nothingness emerges as a something, which his poetry records. But in these leftovers of a plot, the appearance of stoically carrying on, there is a silent scream: it should all be different. Such nihilism implies the very opposite of an identification with nothingness. In a Gnostic way it understands the created world as radically evil, and its negation harbors the possibility of a different world, one that does not yet exist. As long as the world is what it is, all images of reconciliation, peace, and quiet resemble the image of death. The refuge of hope would be the minute difference between nothing and the one finding rest, a no-man's-land between the boundaries of Being and Nothing.[87]

In this passage from *Negative Dialectics*, Adorno again presents a Marcionite argument, i.e., a *theological*, though heterodox, argument; it begins with *Auschwitz* and is oriented towards *Auschwitz*. As Adorno interprets Beckett's screaming silence on the concentration camps as obedience to the biblical commandment against idols, Auschwitz becomes the true place of God, and so God becomes *untrue*: the created world is "radically evil," but its negation is "the possibility of a different world, one that does not yet exist."—"Perhaps the more profound reason for what I have tried to describe as the constituent negativity of the new art is that, unlike horror or absolute negativity, the artwork's motif of 'what has not yet been' cannot be experienced; it is a utopia, beyond experience, it is nothing. In Beckett all these motifs culminate."[88]

---

86. Adorno, *Negative Dialektik*, 372.

87. Ibid., 371–72; recently to be mentioned: Pierre Temkine, *Warten auf Godot. Das Absurde und die Geschichte* (Berlin: Matthes & Seitz, 2008).

88. Adorno, *Vorlesungen zur Ästhetik*, 73; Adorno's numerous Beckett studies and preparatory notes are collated in the *Frankfurter Adorno Blätter III*, edited by Rolf Tiedemann, Theodor W. Adorno Archiv (Frankfurt: edition text + kritik, 1994).

This passage from the *Lectures* also had to be cited, because a question from the audience was the occasion for Adorno to clarify his definition of the relationship between modern art and negative theology in terms of the philosophy of history:

> The place of theological imagination in history is strangely reversed. Once, the Enlightenment wanted to critique religion and art, because religion was merely the horrific fear of fate. Today, art is equally an expression of fear, in the same way myths used to be, but this fear is of the opposite kind. It is a fear of the absence of a metaphysical essence, the expression of a *horror vacui*. This reversal, this metaphysical experience, which is inseparable from inner-worldly, historical experience, marks the decisive turning point in modern art.[89]

After that Adorno *ontologically* sharpens his sociological thesis that "this metaphysical experience . . . is inseparable from inner-worldly, historical experience": "Today, even the claim that the world could be conceived as meaningful is pure mockery. In this sense, I understand . . . what has happened as a *factum* of all-decisive importance. This world now makes a fool of any art that attempts to portray it in a meaningful way. The claim that we live in a meaningful world is no more than an apologetic, defensive reflex. This moment of a lie is deeply engrained in art, and the present crisis of art only sues for a debt which art has shouldered from its very inception."[90]

For our context, the metaphysical quality of the "*factum*" Auschwitz is decisive. That this ontic being—as Günther Anders has said about the *factum* "Hiroshima"[91]—has become *ontological* is the 'a postiori' of *the* 'a priori.'[92] Only by starting from this a posteriori, one can understand Adorno's famous dictum that "to write poetry after Auschwitz is barbaric." He never wanted to "tone it down." As he writes, "The impulse, which [in principle correctly so] inspires socially engaged poetry, is negatively expressed in this way. The question . . . whether art is still permitted at all; whether mental regression as part of the concept of socially engaged literature is not mandated by society's own regression. But [Martin] Enzensberger's reply also holds true," as Adorno is convinced, "which is that poetry has to bear

---

89. Adorno, *Vorlesungen zur Ästhetik*, 74.

90. Ibid., 74, 76.

91. Günther Anders, *Die atomare Bedrohung. Radikale Überlegungen*, 2nd ed. (Munich: Beck, 1981), 173ff.

92. Regarding Auschwitz, cf. also Th. W. Adorno, *Metaphysik*, 160ff., 181ff., and 194ff.

Humilitas qua Sublimitas

this verdict; that is, it should not surrender itself to cynicism merely by virtue of its own existence after Auschwitz. Its own situation is paradox, not only our reaction to it. The excess of real suffering permits no forgetting; Pascal's theological words *'On ne doit plus dormir'* must be secularized. But that suffering, in Hegel's words 'the awareness of sorrow,' also captures the continued existence of art, which it prohibits."[93] It is the continued existence of an art which—in contrast to "socially committed" art—gains "social content" not "in a literal sense . . . but in a modified, cropped, ephemeral sense";[94] and as such it is authentic.

Adorno openly pledged himself to *hermetic* art. So it is even more regrettable that his essay on Paul Celan was never written. From early on, Celan was convinced: "In the midst of all losses, this one thing remains within reach, close at hand, and never lost: language. Yes, despite everything, language remains and is never lost. But now it had to go through its own failure to give answers, had to go through a horrific silence, had to go through the thousand darknesses of death-harboring speech."[95] Peter Szondi then seconded his friend Celan with a sentence dialectically appropriating Adorno: "After Auschwitz no poem is possible, unless it is because of Auschwitz."[96] It is the Auschwitz that, according to Dan Diner, represents "the real crucifixion."[97]

This "crucifixion," which infinitely surpasses that of Jesus of Nazareth, led to such a simplification of style—for example in Beckett—that *humilitas*, more than ever, turned into *sublimitas*, even into *hermeticism* and *enigmatism*. (It would be most interesting to read Auerbach drawing the line from Virginia Woolf and James Joyce to Beckett, and others.[98] It is

---

93. Adorno, *Noten zur Literatur III*, 125–26.

94. Theodor W. Adorno, *Ästhetische Theorie* (Frankfurt: Suhrkamp, 1973), 459.

95. Paul Celan, "Ansprache anläßlich der Entgegennahme des Literaturpreises der Freien Hansestadt Bremen" (26 January 1958), in *Gesammelte Werke*, vol. 3 (Frankfurt: Suhrkamp, 1983), 185–86.

96. Peter Szondi, *Schriften II* (Frankfurt: Suhrkamp, 1978), 384.

97. Dan Diner, "Negative Symbiose. Deutsche und Juden nach Auschwitz," *Babylon: Beiträge zur jüdischen Gegenwart* 1 (1986), 15.

98. Regarding interpretations of Beckett by Günther Anders, mentioned above, see Anders, *Die Antiquiertheit des Menschen*, vol. 1 (Munich: Beck, 1980), 216ff., and also Faber, "*Sagen lassen sich die Menschen nichts, aber erzählen lassen sie sich alles,*" Conclusion (119ff.). For "post-surrealism's," especially Antoine Artaud's relationship to gnosis, I refer (as did Karlheinz Barck) to an essay by Taubes's student Susan Sontag, "Annäherung an Artaud," in Sontag, *Im Zeichen des Saturn. Essays* (Munich: Hanser, 1981), 41–93. ["Approaching Artaud," *The New Yorker*, May 19, 1973, 39ff.]

quite likely he would have drawn attention to Beckett's inheritance of the medieval mystery plays, especially the passion plays.[99] Regarding *Waiting for Godot*, would he have drawn attention to Beckett's negative, or rather desperate Marcionism, waiting in vain for an [alien] god yet to come? We will never know . . .

---

99. I'm grateful to Gerd Poppenberg for pointing out this "inheritance" to me.

II

Atheism in Christianity— Christianity in Atheism

Ernst Bloch's Revolutionary Marcionism[1]

For Francesca Vidal

1. A POLAR DIFFERENTIATION IN THE CONCEPT OF ATHEISM

> My soul does magnify the Lord: And my spirit has rejoiced in God my Savior. For He has regarded the lowliness of His handmaiden. For behold, from henceforth, all generations shall call me blessed. For He that is mighty has magnified me: and holy is His Name. And His mercy is on them that fear him: throughout all generations. He has shown strength with his arm: He has scattered the proud in the imagination of their hearts. He has put down the

---

1. With a few exceptions, Bloch will be cited in the text as follows: A = *Atheismus im Christentum: Zur Religion des Exodus und des Reichs* (Frankfurt: Suhrkamp, 1968), and H = *Das Prinzip Hoffung* (Frankfurt: Suhrkamp, 1967). I thank Martin Leutzsch, Francesca Vidal, and Karlheinz Weigand for their bibliographical recommendations.

mighty from their seat, and has exalted the humble and meek. He has filled the hungry with good things: and the rich He has sent empty away. He, remembering his mercy, has helped His servant Israel, as He promised to our forefathers, Abraham and his seed forever.

Now immersed in a book with the seemingly absurd title *Atheism in Christianity*, the reader should be hardly surprised to be confronted with a lengthy Bible quote (even though this one surprisingly does not appear in Ernst Bloch[2]). But of all possibilities: why this Marian hymn, the Magnificat? Claudio Monteverdi, Johann Sebastian Bach, and others may have splendidly set it to music, but isn't the Marian in itself sugary and kitschy, *eo ipso* folk-religious, Catholic? It is hard to believe, but for the French arch-fascist Charles Maurras, a "condisciple" of Friedrich Nietzsche,[3] Luke 1:46–55 was his main piece of evidence in his relentless trial against Christianity.

The thought, "Well, of course, the text is Jewish through and through," may occur to those who have heard of this Maurras, a prominent anti-Dreyfusard and Nazi collaborator,[4] and of his vehement, ultimately eliminatory anti-Semitism.

"He, remembering his mercy, has helped His servant Israel, as He promised to our forefathers, Abraham and his seed forever." If, according to Maurras, this final passage of the Magnificat is usually not taken seriously—because of people's cultural and religious sloppiness—then even less so is the passage central to him, this *anti-liberal* and *anti-socialist*:[5] "He has shown strength with His arm: He has scattered the proud in the imagination of their hearts. He has put down the mighty from their seat, and has exalted the humble and meek. He has filled the hungry with good things: and the rich He has sent empty away." Above all, in light of these supposedly anarchist verses, Maurras talked about "the poison of the Magnificat"[6] and declared "Judaeo-Christianity" to be the root cause of all modern evils.

2. Cf. at least H, 1482.

3. Cf. Ernst Nolte, *Der Faschismus in seiner Epoche: die Action française, der italienische Faschismus, der Nationalsozialismus*, 2nd ed. (Munich: Piper, 1965), 257.

4. Cf. Richard Faber, "Religiöse, laizistische und neureligiöse (Anti-)Intellektuelle: Ansätze zu einer Realtypologie," in *Völkische Religion und Krisen der Moderne: Entwürfe 'arteigener' Glaubenssysteme seit der Jahrhundertwende*, edited by Stefanie v. Schnurbein and Justus H. Ulbricht (Würzburg: Königshausen & Neumann, 2001), 108–10.

5. Cf. ibid.

6. Cf. Nolte, *Der Faschismus in seiner Epoche*, 170.

(Alain de Benoist, the chief ideologue of the French New Right, still does so today.[7])

Like some anti-clerical freethinker or Marxist, Maurras went so far in his extremism as to profess to be a militant atheist.[8] One irony is that, unlike all of the 'Left,' beginning with the Deist Voltaire, Maurras did so not for humane and humanist reasons, but for decisively inhumane and anti-humanist ones.[9] The other irony, no less remarkable, is that this counter-revolutionary and in the end fascist atheist Maurras was highly interested[10] in forging a political alliance with the mainly anti-democratic Catholicism of the late nineteenth and early twentieth century—itself a kind of natural enemy of the secularist Republic. Still, he loudly proclaimed his atheism on anti-Jewish and anti-Christian grounds—"Catholicism without Christianity," as Robert Spaemann put the Maurrasian paradox in a nutshell.[11]

As Maurras himself put it: "*Je suis athée, mais je suis catholique.*" He chose this phrasing in light of an atheism which had been largely left-wing up to that point. But towards Catholicism, as Christian as ever, the reversal was appropriate: "I am (also) a Catholic, but I'm (at the same time) an atheist." In polar opposition to Maurras, Bloch explicitly condensed his "Atheism in Christianity" into a double formula: "Only an atheist can be a good Christian, only a Christian can be a good atheist" (A, 15). Most briefly, the main task of my presentation may be described as the exegesis of this apparent double paradox. But I would like to further emphasize this quest for "differentiations in the concept of atheism,"[12] the polar tension between Maurras and Bloch, and share the following anecdote:

---

7. Cf. Alain de Benoist, *Heide sein: Zu einem Neuen Anfang; die europäische Glaubensalternative* (Tübingen: Grabert, 1982); critical: K. Kriener, "Julfest versus Christfest: Über das politische 'Heidentum' Alain de Benoists," in *Politische Weihnacht in Antike und Moderne: Zur ideologischen Durchdringung des Fests der Feste*, edited by Richard Faber and Esther Gajek (Würzburg: Königshausen & Neumann, 1997), 141–64.

8. Cf. Richard Faber, "Religiöse, laizistische und neureligiöse (Anti-)Intellektuelle," 108.

9. On anti-humanism in general, see *Streit um den Humanismus*, edited by Richard Faber (Würzburg: Königshausen & Neumann, 2003), chapter 3.

10. Cf. Faber, "Religiöse, laizistische und neureligiöse (Anti-)Intellektuelle," 108–11.

11. Robert Spaemann, "'Politik zuerst'? Das Schicksal der Action Française," *Wort und Wahrheit* 8 (1953), 655ff.

12. I am applying Bloch's lecture title: "Differenzierungen im Begriff Fortschritt" [Differentiations in the Concept of Progress], in *Sitzungsberichte der Deutschen Akademie der Wissenschaften zu Berlin: Klasse für Philosophie*, H. 5, 1955.

In the early years of the war Helmut Gollwitzer—pastor in Berlin-Dahlem after Martin Niemöller's arrest—was once paid a visit by a communist hiding underground. Hardly surprisingly, their talk was mostly about the Nazis. But suddenly the communist made an astonishing remark: the Nazis, said the Marxist full of 'holy wrath', were "godless pagans." Gollwitzer could do nothing but agree, but (in all politeness) had to submit that such a formulation, coming out of the mouth of a dedicated and surely atheist communist, sounded rather peculiar. His interlocutor was unusually confident, waved his hand slightly, and explained that he fully understood what Gollwitzer was saying. But he said that his atheism and the atheism of the Nazis were two completely different things. Gollwitzer remained convinced by this formulation until the end of his life (as a professor at Freie Universität Berlin)—though probably not in the sense that the Nazis were simply devils and the communists angels.

2. NOT A NEO-PAGANISM

Gollwitzer's writing directly engages with Bloch's "Atheism in Christianity," yet always with the greatest respect.[13] As a theologian in the literal, theist sense, he had to do so, though here I cannot expound on the reasons why. Rather, I am interested in the almost identical confrontation of the two with fascism, particularly *in religionibus*: their defense against what Gollwitzer's visitor during that fascist night had called "godless (neo-)paganism." From the perspective of religious studies, this approach is not unproblematic,[14] but in view of the discourse still popular today, it is understandable, even vivid. As late as 1968, Bloch again writes in his *Atheism in Christianity* "that fascist scoundrels like Alfred Rosenberg were selling cheap swill under that label [of metaphysics],[15] and fascist abetters like C. G. Jung or Ludwig Klages were selling what was earthy these days"—which effectively means neo-pagan: "neo" stands for "these days" and "pagan" for "earthy."[16] Bloch,

---

13. Cf. Helmut Gollwitzer, "Die Bibel—marxistisch gelesen." *Verkündigung und Forschung* 14 (1969), 2–37, as well as Gollwitzer, *Krummes Holz—aufrechter Gang: Zur Frage nach dem Sinn des Lebens* (Munich: Kaiser, 1970).

14. Cf. Richard Faber, "'Pagan' und 'Neo-Paganismus,'" in *Die Restauration der Götter: Antike Religion und Neo-Paganismus*, edited by R. Faber and R. Schlesier (Würzburg: Königshausen & Neumann, 1986), 10–25.

15. *[Faber's insertion].

16. Cf. also Richard Faber, "Salzburg—Land der Perchten. Ein Syndrom des Urigen" In *Salzburg: Blicke*, edited by Helga Embacher et al.(Salzburg: Residenz-Verlag 1999),

like his unofficial students Paul Tillich and Theodor W. Adorno,[17] was a decisive opponent of myths of origins, indeed of all genealogical thinking: "Whatever there was, it has to be examined. It is not valid by virtue of itself; it is perhaps familiar, but it lies behind us. It is only valid in so far and in as much as the Where-to lying before us is alive, or not, in what has become. If what is binding backwards has become false, then the tie that binds us has to be cut. And even more so if it was false from the beginning, true only as a shackle" (A, 115).

Unsurprisingly, in Bloch, the utopian thinker of the future, the decisive criterion of truth is the "Where-to before us," which he also calls "the Tomorrow within today," as a "true meta" (A, 96). Hans-Jürgen Krahl quite followed Bloch's meaning, when, eye to eye with Martin Heidegger and only a year after the publication of *Atheism*, he declared: "The anti-ontological concept of *alaetheia*—that is: the Messiah—is the past of present generations as the departure from the origin."[18] It is "significant" already for Bloch, and explicitly so in the sense of the Old Testament, "that the faithful Ruth did not return to where she came from; she did not turn back, but went to where she belonged of her own choosing" (A, 115): to the Jew Boas, with whom together she, the woman from Moabit, became the ancestress of David and Jesus.[19]

It is only logical that Bloch then talks about Jesus himself, not as a Messiah—who cannot possibly exist—but as a great messianic "sign" (A, 169), a sort of Jewish-Christian "seal of the prophets."[20] Also for Bloch: "... how strangely even Jesus' goodness at this point (of origin, or of future) swings to the other side, to that of departure. How disconnected, even as the natural son, he feels from the old home and obedience. He has surpassed it, has cast off its spell, none of it hangs above him anymore. The old

---

175–79.

17. Cf. above all Theodor W. Adorno, *Zur Metakritik der Erkenntnistheorie* (Frankfurt: Suhrkamp, 1971), especially 12–47: "The Concept of a Philosophy of Origin" [*Begriff der Ursprungsphilosophie*].

18. Hans-Jürgen Krahl, *Konstitution und Klassenkampf: Zur historischen Dialektik von bürgerlicher Emanzipation und proletarischer Revolution* (Frankfurt: Verlag Neue Kritik, 1971), 358.

19. Extensively: Jürgen Ebach, "Fremde in Moab—Fremde aus Moab: Das Buch Ruth als politische Literatur." In *Bibel und Literatur*, edited by Jürgen Ebach and Richard Faber (Munich: Fink, 1995), 277–304.

20. Cf. Carsten Colpe, *Das Siegel der Propheten: Historische Beziehungen zwischen Judentum, Judenchristentum, Heidentum und frühem Islam* (Berlin: Inst. Kirche u. Judentum Berlin, 1990).

Father-I itself breaks away, as a newborn he stands here with others just like him, leaving behind father and mother" (A, 115).

Up to this point, the messianic Jesus is an important ally, not only in the anti-fascist struggle. Quite a different matter is the crucified one as a hero in the "pagan" sense. Bloch understands the contemporary sacralization of human sacrifice as a regression back to an era before the humanization of religion, as it was scripted and realized in principle by the prophets:

> Even animal sacrifices were, seven hundred years before Jesus, unforgettably attacked by Amos, this oldest of the prophets (Amos 5:22), and later by Hosea: "For I desired mercy, and not sacrifice; and the knowledge of God more than burnt offerings" (Hosea 6:6) ... And even more so human sacrifices: since the sacrifice of Isaac had been rejected ... human sacrifices ... had a bad liturgical conscience. "And Abraham called the name of that place Jĕ-hō-vă-jī-rēh as it is said to this day, In the mount of the Lord it shall be seen" (Gen 22:14); the Golgotha of the Pauline sacrificial death takes this mountain back, along with the prophets.

And it lets—which is consistent, but nonetheless terrible—the "long forgotten, or at least no longer worshipped, cannibal in heaven" raise another Moloch, "satisfactorily accepting Jesus' self-sacrifice. It was for a reason that this teaching of sacrificial death," Bloch continues, "led Marcion, otherwise a great admirer of Paul, to a reversed faith in Yahweh, meaning: Jesus may have died as a sacrifice, but as one 'of a murderer from the very beginning,' of evil in the world" (A, 223).

Like other German-Jewish philosophers—Walter Benjamin, Theodor W. Adorno, Herbert Marcuse, and Jacob Taubes—Bloch was a "modern Marcionite";[21] Gollwitzer, Taubes's Evangelical-Protestant colleague close by at the Freie Universität, could hardly have been a Marcionite, integral Pauline and Barthian that he was. As a master student of "such a firm antifascist" as Karl Barth, Gollwitzer owed himself to a *totaliter aliter* that was

---

21. Cf. Jacob Taubes, "Walter Benjamin—ein moderner Marcionit?," in *Antike und Moderne: Zu Walter Benjamins "Passagen,"* edited by Norbert W. Bolz and Richard Faber (Würzburg: Königshausen & Neumann, 1986), 138–47, as well as his *Vom Kult zur Kultur* (Munich: Fink 1996), chapter 2, and "Revolution und Transzendenz: Zum Tode des Philosophen Herbert Marcuse," *Der Tagesspiegel*, no. 10290 (31.07.1979), 9; concerning Adorno, see his *Negative Dialektik*, pirated copy, 371—2, and *Metaphysik: Begriff und Probleme* (1965), edited by Rolf Tiedemann (Frankfurt: Suhrkamp, 1998), 235. Secondary literature to be mentioned is, among others, Thomas Ruster, *Der verwechselbare Gott: Theologie nach der Entflechtung von Christentum und Religion*, 4th ed. (Freiburg i. Br.: Herder, 2000).

altogether different from the neo-pagan *totaliter aliter* of the phenomenologist of religion, Rudolf Otto.[22] Gollwitzer's "mysterious Numinous" had nothing to do with that of Otto. Of course for Otto, "the religious" was "tied as closely as possible to the shudder of myth—also in the Bible. Hence even Christian meekness was drawn into the pagan Rough Night;[23] it was now called 'mysterium fascinosum', and could see itself as equally mysterious besides the 'mysterium tremendum' of the old God of Thunder—that is, it could not be seen" (A, 73): it could be seen no longer in the fascist Rough Night arising for real in town and country. This is what Bloch alludes to[24] when he indirectly quotes himself:

"Today ... town and country are both becoming a superstition; in the towns too, the earth has been victorious over movement, and so has a very old space been victorious over time.... Despairing people are wearing animal masks, the way only drunken peasants do during Bavarian-Austrian Rough Night; rutting season with a grimace appears as Advent." Already in 1929 Bloch shrewdly saw what lay ahead. In the essay "Amusement Co., Horror, Third Reich," dated September 1930, the month of a great electoral success for the National Socialists, he writes:

> the old grimaces are rising like ghosts, but they are real: like the Nazi who, clad in yellow fur down to his feet, danced in front of Böss's house upon his arrival; five hundred years ago, when Jews were clubbed to death, he used to be just as wild and funny. He danced with a fur skin, swinging and raging all night, because Böss, the mayor of Berlin, was also involved in a scandal to do with fur. But the stench of this performance is ancient, despite its miserable joke, the shabby stupidity of its allusion; it is ancient and horrific, as if from a nightmare and the abysses it touches on.[25]

---

22. Cf. Rudolf Otto, *Das Heilige: Über das Irrationale in der Idee des Göttlichen und sein Verhältnis zum Rationalen,* 11th ed. (Stuttgart/Gotha: Frdr. Andreas Perthes, 1923); critical is, amongst others, R. Flasche, "Religionsmodelle und Erkenntnisprinzipien der Religionswissenschaft in der Weimarer Zeit." In *Religions und Geistesgeschichte der Weimarer Republik,* edited by Hubert Cancik (Düsseldorf: Patmos-Verlag, 1982), 261–76.

23. *Translators' note: [*Rauhnacht*]: the nights around the New Year during which, according to Germanic myths, the realm of spirits opens up. Through processions involving demon and animal masks, bells, and other loud noise, evil spirits are exorcised.

24. More extensively: Richard Faber, *Erbschaft jener Zeit: Zu Ernst Bloch und Hermann Broch* (Würzburg: Königshausen & Neumann, 1989).

25. Ernst Bloch, *Erbschaft dieser Zeit* (Frankfurt: Suhrkamp, 1973), 57–58 and 62.

This Nazi, so particularly agile against the left-liberal mayor of Berlin, is an "ancient" figure, but—as Bloch saw as early as 1929—only "this time the employees of the town ... are crossing the ditches of arrogance between town and country," and now they are letting the "myth of the earth into their world": "Only now, as for the peasants, the Jew has invented the crisis; indeed the crisis, capitalism, and Marxism are identified with fantastical, even fantastically intentional ignorance; the town turns itself into rubble. In all its ruins one can see today how far"—here he freely adapts Ludwig Klages—"the instinctive 'drive' is out on the loose against the 'spirit,' the blood drive, the drive of the wild, which is the only 'country' of town people."[26]

The large city's reaction "regresses as far as ... the berserker and his dark rampage." This berserker marches "in every direction ... where destruction is to be wrought," as Bloch repeats in the essay on Böss, "Amusement Co., Horror, Third Reich." In any case, "the emptiness of amusement (which nobody had believed in ...)" has become the emptiness "of intoxication ... with the exotic at home, with a national myth (which the National Socialist certainly believes in); it is filled with kitsch and a myth that does not have its fantasies in the distance, but rather in the vertical, so to speak, right underneath the ground of home"—meaning the Germanic home.[27]

3. A HUMANIST, MATERIALIST, AND SOCIALIST ATHEISM

So much for Bloch's confrontation with the *völkisch* and ultimately National-Socialist neopaganism on political and humane grounds. His response implied a partial apology for Christianity, though not just for the sake of "political alliances" with the Volksfront[28] strategy he shared.[29] Already with regard to Nietzsche, for whom he often expresses high esteem,[30] Bloch had

26. Ibid., 57.

27. Ibid., 60, 65, and 59.

28. *Translators' note: *Deutsche Volksfront*: a resistance group founded in 1936 with members from the Communist and Social Democratic parties; it was broken up by the Nazis in 1938.

29. Cf. Richard Faber, "Ernst Bloch und das Hambacher 'Fest der Hoffnung'" In *Liberalismus in Geschichte und Gegenwart*, edited by Faber (Würzburg: Königshausen &Neumann, 2000), 21–37, especially, 30–33.

30. Cf., amongst others, Hanna Gekle, "Utopisches Versprechen irdischer Glückseligkeit: Ernst Blochs Rezeption der Antike." In *Antike heute*, edited by Faber and Bernhard Kytzler (Würzburg: Königshausen & Neumann: 1992), 216–37.

rejected the confusion between atheism and anti-Christianity (A, 323): "an atheist who has understood that everything conceived under God is really an instruction for a human content which has not yet appeared, is not an atheist" (H, 1527). But at the same time there can be no doubt about Bloch's own, humanist atheism. According to an episode in his autobiography, he was only thirteen years old when, during his confirmation ceremony, he provoked his baffled relatives and the Ludwigshafen clergy by shouting several times in the direction of the surrounding guests: "I'm an atheist!" He recalls, "I pronounced the ei as a diphthong; we had always only read, but never heard the word."[31]

Moreover, in the chapter entitled "God as the Utopically Hypostasized Ideal of the Unknown Man" one may find the categorical statement "all mythology of a being in view of a divine, all theology as science proper has been done away with. However, what has not been done away with," Bloch adds, simultaneously furthering both Hegel and Feuerbach, "is what is conceived as divine, towards the side of its hope and non-alienation, the content of its hope not yet relinquished to heaven" (H, 1515–16).

And conversely: if religions do not leave the ultimate absolute open as a utopia and always order humanity towards it, but if instead they cover its topos through God's or gods' hypostasis, then there is no hope precisely where there is religion;[32] where there is "re-ligio," a "re-connection, specifically with a mythical God of the beginning, the creation of the world; . . . the received Exodus-confession of 'I am, who I am.'" For Bloch, however, "even confessing the Christianity of the Son of Man and the eschaton," is "no [such] religion anymore" (A, 15); "because what the numinous [of religion] promised, the Messianic aims to keep: its humanum and the world adequate to it are . . . the distant shore in the early light of dawn . . . .'" Bloch is convinced that "The aim of all higher religions was a land where milk and honey flow, in reality as much as symbolically; the aim of an atheism with content, which is left after the religions, is precisely the same—without God, but with the uncovered face of our absconditum and the salvific latency in this difficult earth" (H, 1415, 1550).

31. Cf. Ernst Bloch, *Spuren* (Frankfurt: Suhrkamp, 1959), 82; as well as Arno Münster, "Ernst Blochs Religionsphilosophie im Spannungsfeld von jüdischem Messianismus: ketzerischen Christentum und materialistischem Atheismus." In *VorSchein. Jb. der Ernst-Bloch-Assoziation* 22–23 (2002), 49.

32. Cf. Elke Kruttschnitt, *Ernst Bloch und das Christentum: der geschichtliche Prozeß und der philosophische Begriff der "Religion des Exodus und des Reichs"* (Mainz: M. Grünewald, 1993), 312.

Bloch here speaks about the "uncovered face of our absconditum" in a meta-Feuerbachian way, and simultaneously as a meta-Hegelian, or rather a Marxist, about "the salvific latency in this difficult earth." Therefore let us first look at "this so-very-important atheist" Feuerbach; "with him the final story of Christianity begins. Not only did he want to be the undertaker of traditional religion—an easy office one hundred years after Voltaire and Diderot. More than that, he was gripped by the problem of religious inheritance" (H, 1519); Bloch himself was too, being an anthropologist and indeed a humanist. Bloch cites also Karl Marx, with whom he agrees: "Atheism is humanism mediated by the [Feuerbachian] sublation of religion." And he explicates that Feuerbach's atheism was "conceived as the destruction of an annoying illusion . . . as well as the encouraging re-transformation of theological limitations back into human ones at last" (A, 87, 282). Certainly, at the same time Bloch 'meta-criticizes' Feuerbach for knowing "the human being, the doubled subject in religion, only in the way it has appeared in existence so far, and this existence only as an abstractly stable one, the so-called species–being of the human. What is lacking . . . is its non-finality. In the shallowness of the bourgeois human, which Feuerbach has absolutized, there is definitely no space for the religious contents . . . And in the least . . . the religious images blasting all status . . . , the chiliastic images of 'Behold, I make all things new' and of the Kingdom." For Bloch, "Evidently . . . only openness of the subject and his world is capable of taking up again the anticipation of absolute perfection in the same way it has posited it outside of itself. Hence, if religion is to be anthropologized, Feuerbach's anthropologization presupposes a utopian concept of the human being, not a static completed one. Equally it presupposes a homo absconditus, like the belief in heaven always contained a Deus absconditus, a hidden, latent God" (H, 1517–18).

The wholly Other of that God then is, in view of his "human transformation (formation of kingdom),[33] no longer the Other, but the Actual that was longed for" (H, 1417), as Bloch defines his own radical humanist position, adapting both Barth and Otto. What is desperately needed is a utopian anthropology: a "transcending without all heavenly transcendence, but with an understanding of it: as a hypostasized presumption of its being for itself" (H, 1522).

Bloch is convinced that "no humanism able to be carried out" can exist, "unless beyond its morality it also implies . . . the happiest border

---

33. [Reich].

images of the Where-to, What-for, At-All ... [But] their freedom lies in the elongation of the homo absconditus not yet brought out in the world" (A, 352-13). Or to put it in other words, freedom lies in the uncovering of the hidden, human "face," by which is meant "our always intended identity itself, not only in an eschatological, but apocalyptic, i.e., un-covering sense," precisely "as the Kingdom of the Son of Man everywhere. The ancient 'Day of Yahweh' at the end of time ... in the fourth Gospel is set up as a parousia of Christ, that is, the Son of Man who is without Yahweh, really A-Kyrios and A-Theos at the same time." As "it says accordingly elsewhere [in Bloch]: 'The truth of the ideal of God is solely the utopia of the Kingdom; its presupposition is precisely that there is no God up on high, that there is none, nor was there ever one.' (*Das Prinzip Hoffnung*, 1959, p. 1514)" (A, 218).

So the biblical key words of Bloch's utopianization of Feuerbach's anthropology are the Son of Man and his Kingdom, whereby Bloch (by this point quite unsurprisingly) reads the Son of Man "instead of the Son of God" and in consequence understands Kingdom as a human kingdom "of freedom" (A, 190). Indeed the Son of Man, whose "power and figure" is "the final one, overcoming all" (A, 191), had posited himself—eschatologically (A, 207)—"in God as a human" (A, 183), thus realising the "*Eritis sicut deus*" of the paradisiacal snake.

This "*Eritis sicut deus*" for Bloch is the "Good News of Christian salvation" (H, 1504). Humans turn out so well in the Bible, "indeed much better than anywhere else" (A, 191). Bloch talks about the "transhumanization ... of God" (H, 1487) by the Son of Man Jesus; in this way he also articulates his own transcending of Feuerbach: "The religion of the gathering kingdom ... does not call the divine back in under well-known human standards ...; on the contrary, the Son of Man and his space are [still] human—*not yet given*. They stand askew in relation to the existing figure of the subject, as much as they stand askew in relation to the gigantic measures of the existing cosmos" (A, 205–6).

At the end here this is once again the ontologist speaking, or rather the cosmologist or Marxist materialist indebted to Hegel, but in any case the natural philosopher Bloch. And down to the original terms of on/ontos, cosmos, materia, and natura he is indebted to Greek-Roman antiquity. Indeed he makes no secret of it; "creation ex nihilo" and world escapism (whether addicted to death or heaven) was never his thing anyway. Certainly he always presumes that in a Bible not yet dogmatized and therefore *manipulated*—including Christian dogma and manipulation—the "earthly beautiful life of nature" is not "simply shaken off, but radically transformed" and even "surpassed" (A, 259). In any case he is also highly interested in *its* utopianization or "messianization."

No matter how strong Bloch's inclination towards an arcadian, that is—as is commonly understood—a pagan nature and his taste for its rediscovery by the likes of Goethe, he still protested against the latter's exemplary Spinozism: "This pantheism which is not even aware of its own utopianism" derived "images of happiness from the humanization of an all-nature, as if this *deus sive natura* was already here" (A, 302). "Everything about Pan" for Goethe and his intellectual relatives is supposedly "all in good order" (A, 301), already now, *rebus sic stantibus*. But this could hardly be the case. "The no longer alienated humanum, the not-yet-found of its possible world—both lie necessarily in the experiment of *future*, the *experiment* of World" (A, 354). With these words Bloch's *Atheism*-book closes.

And it is with these sentences that the 1628-page-long *Principle of Hope* closes: "Humanity everywhere still lives in"—as Marx called it—"prehistory, indeed everything has"—in the words of a paradoxical theology of creation—"the creation of the world still ahead of itself, as a just world. *True Genesis is not at the beginning, but in the end*." This is a thesis Bloch italicizes: "and it only starts to begin when society and existence become radical, that is, they take themselves by their roots. The root of history, however, is"—again this is Marxist—"the human being, who works, creates, reshapes, and overcomes present realities. Once he has grasped himself and has founded what is his own in a real democracy, without divestment and without alienation, something will come into the world that shines into everyone's childhood, but where no one has ever been: home" (H, 1628). An *earthly*, not a heavenly home, as we need not emphasize again.

New (for us) is Bloch's departure into the social and political dimension of his "real," as it were, *materialist* humanism: "Suffering no longer . . . teaches us to pray, simply because most of it is caused and brought upon us by humans *like us*" (A, 37), as it says in *Atheism in Christianity*. Emphasizing in this atheism the a- (or rather the *anti*-) monarchic, *anti*-monarchist, he writes of "an above which is deaf . . . for most people never became such an above; the king's messengers on horseback hardly ever turn up, and kings in general are not the custom anymore. Even in places where the Enlightenment did not take hold so much, the old feeling ceases or is still only paid lip service. The experience of the Father–I in the family is almost gone, and hence also its projection into a high above. In almost all the states it is still the case that there is no longer a throne, neither is there a projection of it, which would fill the gaps of earthly needs and explanations with additional supernatural weight" (A, 38).

Instead of monarchy, democracy is the order of the day, and for that matter as a "real" one: "Humanity finds space in a democracy truly made possible, in the same way that this democracy itself is the first humane place to live" (H, 1608). It is simultaneously the space that, in Bloch's understanding of Christianity, is truly Christian, akin to the *Son of Man*. Because for Bloch "only in later Hellenic Christianity the Kyrios Christos, venerated like a god of the imperial cult, appeared beside, and even instead of, the figure of the imminently coming Son of Man. And . . . what remained for the poor, those who rebelled from the inside and above all on the outside against everything above, where there is no human being," was "the figure of the Son of Man": "for the heretical brothers of good will, of common life, of full spirit, of free spirit, for Thomas Münzer and his Allstedt sermon about the Son of Man's face in the Book of Daniel and the true cornerstone Jesus, whom the builders have rejected" (A, 211).

4. SOCIAL-REVOLUTIONARY JUDAISM AND CHRISTIANITY

Thomas Münzer, whom Bloch as early as the 1920s celebrated as "the theologian of the *revolution*,"[34] referred back to the Magnificat we cited at the beginning, and he never thought it was an impossibility or even that it was "enthusiasm . . . to bring the godless down from the chair of judgment, and to raise the low and the coarse" (H, 1482). In our context it is decisive that Bloch, extending Münzer's work, puts forward the following thesis: "The Son of Man not only smashed . . . the myth of the Son of God into pieces, but . . . also the myth of his sitting on the throne 'on the right hand of the Father'; now a tribune (of the people) sits there, and so he does away with the throne itself" (A, 227). Despite (or precisely because of) the Roman title "tribune," Christ is a "rebel," "politically straightforwardly . . . against [imperialist] Rome" and all its Euro-American descendants.[35] "The

---

34. Cf. Ernst Bloch, *Thomas Münzer als Theologe der Revolution* (Munich: Kurt Wolff, 1921), 2nd ed. Frankfurt, 1963.

35. Cf. Richard Faber, *Das ewige Rom, oder, die Stadt und der Erdkreis: zur Archäologie "abendländischer" Globalisierung* [Eternal Rome, or, The City and the Globe: On the Archaeology of the "Occidental" Globalization] (Würzburg: Königshausen & Neumann,

Political Demonology

cross is the punishment for *insurgency*," Bloch emphasizes (A, 173). Jesus "was executed by the Romans as an *accuser*," and even further, it was "for a reason" that "the High Priest and the Pharisees" feared "the man ... for whom the whole theocracy of the priests and the religion of the law ... was part of a world ripe for destruction. Such a Jesus was dangerous; it was not necessarily a misunderstanding that, against him and his eschatological radicalism, the interests of the Jewish upper class and the Roman oppressors were aligned," Bloch summarizes (A, 182).

Specifically with regard to the Jewish upper class he gets more *precise*:

> It was deception when the priests appealed to Jesus' having professed to be the son of God, that is the Messiah, and when they said that because of his blasphemy (John 19:7) he would have to die "according to the law" (Lev 24:16). Because even in the century before Jesus ... enthusiasts had appeared who also claimed to be the Messiah, but nothing had happened to them. Similarly, after Jesus there was the hero of the insurgency against Hadrian, Bar Kochba, meaning "Son of the Stars," and such an authority as Rabbi Akiba consecrated him as the Messiah. But Bar Kochba fought ... for the *existing* Judaea, *together with* the rich, the poor, and the priests. He was an insurgent against Rome, but he fought to *preserve* the world of homely tradition, including the priestly tradition of theocracy; so he could be blessed by the priests, and the title of Messiah, unique and awesome, did not count as a blasphemy, as it had with Jesus. With Jesus, by contrast, it was not that he was too peaceful to be given consideration as the Messiah; rather, his kingdom of the Son of Man was too remote from that Master-Yahweh [of the upper class], who re-appeared and re-legitimized himself over and over again, and who had *not* led the people out of Egypt. (A, 182–83)

We will have to come back to the "*Master*-Yahweh" and the Exodus in Bloch's formulations. At this point we will keep the focus on the *non*-peaceability of Bloch's Jesus. "Of course, with the Sermon on the Mount," Bloch at first admits,

> Jesus was not enthusiastically commending to his disciples the incitement of people against each other for Christ's sake (Matt 10:35f.). But rather the Sermon on the Mount, with its blessings of the meek and the peacemakers, refers not to the days of struggle, but to the *end* of time, which Jesus believed to be near ... ; hence

---

2000).

the *immediate*, chiliastic reference to the Kingdom of Heaven (Matt 5:3). Yet for the *struggle*, for *bringing about* the Kingdom there are these words: "I came not to send peace, but a sword." (Matt 10:34)

as well as the related: "I have come to send fire on the earth; and how I wish it were already kindled" (Luke 12:49)! Bloch is convinced, "This is exactly the meaning of William Blake's corollary, applicable to 1789":

> in Blake's verses: "The spirit of turmoil shot down from the Saviour / And in the vineyards of red France appear'd the light of his fury." In Jesus' preaching the sword and the fire, which destroys as much as it purifies, are not merely aimed at palaces; they go against all of the old aeon, which has to pass away. It is spearheaded by the enemies of the weary and the burdened, the rich, who are as likely to go to heaven as—with all the irony of the impossible—a camel is likely to pass through the eye of a needle. Later on the Church widened the eye of the needle so much that Jesus fell out of revolutionary sight. Not the wrath of Jesus but his mildness, even toward the unjust, now became triumphant. But even Kautsky, who saw nothing but "religious mantles" everywhere, had to admit in his *Origin of Christianity*: "Rarely has the modern proletariat's class-hatred taken such fanatical forms as has that of the Christians." And from another side, the very side of the "religious mantle," so *malgré lui* and hence particularly *épatant*, Chesterton [the Catholic priest and author] clarifies the misunderstanding and dispels all pretence of sweet little Jesus and all its resultant ethical demureness and its reforms. In *The Everlasting Man* he chides it in this way: "Those who charged the Christians with burning down Rome with firebrands were slanderers; but they were at least far nearer to the nature of Christianity than those among the moderns who tell us that the Christians were a sort of ethical society, being martyred in a languid fashion for telling men they had a duty to their neighbours, and only mildly disliked because they were meek and mild." (A, 170–71)

And as Bloch glosses Chesterton: "the subversive element of early Christianity unmistakably surfaces in this way" (A, 171), but Chesterton is and remains a witness *malgré lui*. For Bloch the mutinous peasants of almost all European countries are downright witnesses, that is *martyrs*, from the Middle Ages until the Cevennes, "almost 90 years before the French Revolution" (A, 20–21). And a prominent one—an arch-martyr, as it were—is *Thomas Münzer*. This enormously significant theologian not only defied the Catholic and Lutheran "ruler-clerics," but presciently also the "anti-Semitic liberal theologians" of the nineteenth and twentieth centuries who "separated Jesus from the Jewish dream of the Messiah," which "also means from political eschatology" (A, 174).

One cannot overlook for a single moment that Bloch's Jesus, who defied the Jewish *authorities*, was himself *Jewish* through and through: revolutionary as an *apocalyptic prophet*, and finally a Moses redivivus or rather *ultimus*, committed to the Exodus, surpassing and also theologically *perfecting* Moses.[36] Needless to say, in making this claim as Martin Buber also does, Bloch sets himself against those Jews who, like Hermann Cohen, essentially wanted to excommunicate Jesus from Judaism (A, 85–86).

If they want to be consistent, the Jews who are one-sidedly committed to "Rabbinic Orthodoxy" have to ban *all* apocalypticism. In any case, Jesus and some of his followers over the centuries were also apocalypticists. Bloch emphasizes this in a way that, of all Jewish philosophers of religion, only Jacob Taubes emphasized as forcefully. And he emphasizes it again in particular with Thomas Münzer in mind: it had been "for a reason" that "Luther called the final book of the Bible"—the Revelation of St. John—"'the conjuror's bag of all mob leaders," since the eschaton there is neither within it, nor is it an inaccessible taboo—not even as a wild myth—nor does it lack a break from the regional governor, from the father of the world, or from instituted authority. On the contrary, it contains the strongest discontent within all re-ligio, all re-connection; the Advent in it completely lacks an *ordo sempiternus rerum*" (A, 63–64).

There is in Revelation the promise of "a *New* Heaven and a *New* Earth," as Bloch enthusiastically quotes over and over again. Yet within Judaism it is of the utmost significance that this Christian apocalypticism is an heir of an altogether Jewish *propheticism*, in the same way that Jesus himself and everyone else—as I have already mentioned with regard to Jesus—stand on the shoulders of Moses. Amos, the "first prophet," was "a courageous man, embittered about the rich oppressors like no one before him," and yet he has "like Daniel, the last" prophet—or first apocalypticist—"an inheritance as well. Indeed it says (Amos 2:5–7): 'But I will send a fire upon Judah, and it shall devour the palaces of Jerusalem . . .; because they sold the righteous for silver, and the poor for a pair of shoes. That pant after the dust of the earth on the head of the poor, and turn aside the way of the meek'—such a

---

36. Cf. Martin Leutzsch, "Das Jesusbild von Ernst Bloch." *VorSchein. Jb. der Ernst-Bloch-Assoziation* 22/23 (2002), 25.

Atheism in Christianity—Christianity in Atheism

torch, such a 'red rooster on the convent's roof,'[37] had never been lit before," as Bloch glosses.

> And then there is even the world revolution without Yahweh, with a new regent in Daniel (7:13–14): "And behold, one like the Son of Man came with the clouds of heaven, and came to the Ancient of days, and they brought him near before him. And there was given him dominion, and glory, and a kingdom, that all people, nations, and languages should serve him: his dominion is an everlasting dominion which shall not pass away, and his kingdom that which shall not be destroyed." Looking backwards, this mysterious text on the superseding Son of Man is almost all on its own; even in the prophets it is alluded to only in Ezekiel (1:26), never in the books of Moses. And yet the Israelite prophets appeared . . . always in the light of Moses, as if they were none without him. Because the moral command, the promise of the future did not only originate in the prophets, and neither do they leave Moses aside in their older origin or more heated eschaton, for example to replace him with sources from outside Israel. As it was once [around 1900] attempted in a "pan-Babylonian"[38] manner, with the ancient pre-Mosaic book of Hammurabi and, concerning promises of the future, with the supposedly only post-Mosaic messianism from Persia, the teaching of Zoroaster's future return. But both the law of Hammurabi and Persian messianism, appearing only after Isaiah (11:1), lack the memory of a time in slavery, stripped of all rights, of a daring exodus to Canaan—all of this a demolition rather than a trumpeting apotheosis. It is also this permanent resonance of the unique which the prophets possess exclusively in their . . . Moses, and which he sustains in them, however large the break and the leap. (A, 140–41)

To keep it brief: Bloch's *Atheism in Christianity* carries the subtitle "On the Religion of Exodus and Kingdom." It is thus first of all "the *Jewish* Exodus," which is then followed by "the Kingdom that is *also* Christian." Without doubt, the latter perfects the Exodus, and as *specifically* Christian

---

37. *Translators' note: A line in a political folk song after the First World War, *Wir sind des Geyers schwarzer Haufen* (We Are Geyer's Black Mob), referred to Florian Geyer during the German Peasants' War (1524–25): *Setzt aufs Klosterdach den roten Hahn!* ("Put the red rooster on the abbey's roof!" i.e., "Torch that convent down.")

38. *Translators' note: Within Assyriology and Religious Studies, Panbabylonism appeared in the late nineteenth century. It considers the Hebrew Bible and Judaism to be directly derived from Mesopotamian (Babylonian) mythology. It gained popularity in the early twentieth century, advocated by e.g., Alfred Jeremias.

it is also an "Exodus from the God of the Exodus" (H, 1527). However, what binds together the Exodus and the Kingdom [*Reich*] from beginning to end is a *Jewish* messianism. Not only for that reason does "Atheism in Christianity" signify "Atheism in Judaism" as well:

> The utopia of the Kingdom destroys the fiction of a creator god and the hypostasis of a heavenly god, but does not destroy the final space in which the *ens perfectissimum* has an abyss of its still unthwarted latency. The existence of God, God as a general essence as such, is a superstition; real faith is only in a messianic Kingdom of God—without God. Hence atheism is hardly the enemy of religious utopia, because it is its premise: *without atheism there is no room for messianism.* (H, 1413)

Nonetheless, and maybe precisely in that way, this atheism remains messianic: "The truth of the ideal of God is simply the utopia of the Kingdom" (H, 1524). And "an Omega of Christian utopia was nowhere else . . . posited in such a non-transcendent way, while still being most powerfully transcendent (as with the "New Jerusalem" [Rev 21:23]). And even this utopia as "New Canaan" had as its "most central part" "the Omega of 'a free people on a free earth'" (A, 303). Joachim of Fiore (the great high-medieval warrantor for Münzer, Bloch, and Taubes) had long before posited "the true vine of Canaan" "as a historical Omega" (A, 265).

Bloch summarizes, "Item: the dream of the messiah rushes forward . . . from the Exodus," and from its God of the "I am who I am"; "Moses evokes this risen symbol as the 'way out of servitude,' pointing toward a horizon of expectant liberation" (A, 124). But then of course the prophets began, and the last of them, Jesus of Nazareth, completed the "exodus from Pharaoh with the idea of an exodus from Yahweh." Or to be more precise: it was *Marcion*, the heretical disciple of Paul, who completed this prophesied "exodus from Pharaoh with the idea of an exodus from Yahweh"; it was only he who consequently and radically set the savior Son of Man *against* the creator God, indeed played one off against the other: "Marcion represents . . . the strongest concept of Anti-Yahweh, in favor of Christ as the radical Novum, . . . in Yahweh's world. Of course, by tearing down the bridge to the Old Testament, he himself stands on that bridge" (H, 1499). This is the decisive point for our context here. Bloch writes, "Marcion not only starts from Paul, he also starts from Moses; the true or alien God is dawning in the God of the Exodus, between Egypt and Canaan" (H, 1500).

Atheism in Christianity—Christianity in Atheism

But let us first examine more closely the Exodus, that out of Egypt; this exodus breaks with the tradition of the autochthonic, and searches for a homeland through emancipation from the origin, removal from the earth that is not home.[39] But even Canaan would prove to be an unworthy homeland: "The people were freed . . . from lifting bricks. But milk and honey they never got to taste in the holy land, the land so much fought for . . . . The Egyptian masters had only changed names; they were now in the in the Israelite cities, and the estates that had been taken over." Or to calculate the loss:

> As the Israelite Bedouins entered the preformed stratification of rich and poor in Canaan . . . the old, simple life of the tribe, a partly ur-communist life, was lost. The wealth of the few here, as everywhere and in all ages, created the suffering of the many; common wealth disappeared, private property took its place. With it arose the well-known differences between master and slave. Those in debt were sold off into slavery by their creditors, grains were exported at higher prices out of the land by the big landowners, and so a shortage crisis was created at home. The Book of Judges, with its age of heroics, obscures all this. But the two Books of Kings are full of reports of famine and its related opposite: "There was a great inflation in Samaria" (1 Kings 18:2); and then: "The King [Solomon] had it that there was so much silver in Jerusalem as there were stones" (1 Kings 10:27). (A, 126)

In this strongly re-Egyptianized situation, Israel's own God—not a god of land ownership but a god of the migration of peoples—once again came to rescue the exploited impoverished, thanks to the half-nomads who were calling attention back to him. Bloch calls them by the name—at that time current in academic usage—"Nazirites," i.e., "separated," and, if one is not so well-meaning, "sectarian." In any case, these Nazirites "preach nothing less than a new religious dream (under the mask of the old): a return to the old, communal life, Yahweh as a God of the poor." And, as I skip some material here, he points to what is decisive: "few institutions of old, with all their ascetic-'anti-Canaanite' provocative character, have remained standing so consistently throughout the Bible in the way the Nazirite vow has. Samson, Samuel, Elijah were Nazirites (Judges 13:5; 1 Sam 1:11; 2 Kings

---

39. Cf. Norbert Bolz, "Erlösung als ob: Über einige gnostische Motive der Kritischen Theorie," in *Gnosis und Politik*, edited by Jacob Taubes (Munich: Fink, 1984), 264–89, 289.

1:8), but also John the Baptist, this unwieldy figure from the desert" (A, 128).

"Links between the Nazirites . . . and other late Jewish sects of the Anti-Mammon, the Essenes and Ebionites (ebionim: the poor) are uncertain [for Bloch as well]; but what remains certain [for him]: the early Christian communism of love did not spring from the Book of Kings. He could [instead] rely on a tradition in Israel which" went back as far as "the memory of nomadic common property in Nazirism." The key point for Bloch—especially in view of John, Jesus, and the early church—is "the hugely consequential connection of Nazirism and . . . prophecy, that is: the connection of a social sermon and the will of a new Yahweh and his day" (A, 128–129)—"by virtue of an actual turn from . . . the merely archaic to what is listening, judging, hoping" (A, 129); and to accentuate Bloch's meaning here: to the apocalyptic–*Jesuan*.

I shall turn his *divine length* into *diabolic brevity*, if you like. To take away some of its enigmatic character, I will finally present Bloch's own collage made up of "social-moral" sermons from the prophets:

> "Learn to do well; seek judgment, relieve the oppressed, judge the fatherless, plead for the widow" (Isa 1:17). Yahweh detests exploitation and enclosure . . . Sure, private property is no longer fought as the Nazirites had fought it; each and every one is to sit under his own vine and his own fig tree. But this is so that there are no longer slaves and so that no one is smothered before their time. "And I will punish the world for their evil, and the wicked for their iniquity; and I will cause the arrogance of the proud to cease, and will lay low the haughtiness of the terrible. I will make a man more precious than fine gold; even more than the golden wedge of Ophir" (Isa 13:11–12). The God who wants this is certainly not the one for whom churches were and are consecrated in the various Fifth Avenues of the world; but neither is he—by the oath of Thomas Münzer—the opium of the people: "But thus said the Lord, Even the captives of the mighty shall be taken away, and the prey of the terrible shall be delivered: for I will contend with him that contends with you, and I will save your children. And I will feed them that oppress you with their own flesh; and they shall be drunken with their own blood, as with sweet wine: and all flesh shall know what I the Lord am your Savior and your Redeemer, and the mighty One of Jacob" (Isa 49:25–26). So this is the social-moral content in the prophets; it became explosive once and for all with the social-apocalyptically subversive sermon. (A, 131)

as Bloch ends his text collage, which I have slightly shortened, on a Christian note.

5. MODERN MARCIONISM

Once again I would like to bring back to mind Luke 1:46–55, partly because of the churches in the world's various Fifth Avenues mentioned by Bloch. But I shall decelerate Bloch and stress that he still identifies the "will stretching from Amos to Isaiah," which he regards as "arch-humane," as Yahweh's will. Yahweh's role as the *creator* God is of course notably underexposed by the prophets: they show

> remarkably little interest in quotes from Genesis; there is almost an interest to the contrary. Not an interest against "the spirit of God" as creative, but against the pathos of Genesis about the beginning of such an inadequate world, and about a God who even finds his creation very good and passes the blame for everything else on to humans, like scapegoats, even though he has created them as well. And as this very Yahweh, the world's creator and simultaneously its ruler, continues with these powerful-yet-void machinations against humans, particularly against his chosen people, the prophets begin to turn against everything that has essentially come to pass, in short . . . a bringing-to-an-end, an *eschatological* finishing with all this "Egypt," with "Babylon" altogether. Hence Isaiah (43:18): "Remember you not the former things, neither consider the things of old"—all this referring to the degeneration that happened, to the catastrophes of the promise, while never referring to the *deus creato*r who allows such catastrophes, thereby urgently leaving open a future not yet discredited, indeed a promise not yet fulfilled. (A, 144–5)

So as to leave no room for doubt, Bloch once again probes: "Even 'Paradise' before the 'Fall,' to which this 'See, and it was very good' could still refer, seemed . . . so far from perfect, that the 'new Zion' of prophecy could by no means be a mere reconstitution" (A, 146). Theologically, in the narrowest sense of the word, the emphatically *new* Genesis of the end came about with the appearance of the *rescuer*-God Yahweh in place of the old creator-God. Between this last and what was more likely to be a new rescuer, or rather savior, a polar tension developed over time. "Though the extent of this tension" is, at first,

> hardly reflected on, not even in light of the creator's vast omissions (for the sake of the savior). The antithetic consequences of the tearing apart of God may not yet be drawn, in the way they are later in the Book of Job, and as they are much later ... in Marcion, where "our Father, the creator of the world" ... became the enemy ... for the sake of the scheme of Christ the Savior. For all the prophets ... the world of Genesis ... became incriminating for Yahweh; there was still no exodus from him, but there was already an exodus from the heavens, which ... went on praising the works of the Eternal One. (A, 146)

In any case, already in the prophets "the original category of exodus ... continues to ... work," and it does so in a moral way: "Morality was given ... to man as a dangerous standard for measuring the ways of God, whohe was taught"—by the prophets—"was a synonym for justice ... Yahweh as the epitome of moral [*sittlich*] reason. This is," for Bloch, "after the God of Exodus, the second great wishful image of theology ... Justice now ceases to be merely given from above, an exchange mechanism which is supposed to pay out the exact amount of atonement for sinful debt, justice as the reward for righteousness ... But where the connection sin–atonement as an equivalence was nevertheless insisted on, there justice was turned from an apology for Yahweh into a weapon against him" (A, 134–5). With this Bloch arrives at the book of Job.

According to Bloch, in Job began the "Exodus from the idea of Yahweh itself" (A, 152 and 148): a despotic, or rather—already in view of Jesus— "Caesarian idea of God" (A, 165). Here for the first time the human being is set "above every kind of tyranny," "above the questionable one of a justice from above," but "also above the new-mythological one of a majestic nature as such": "The God in Job: known by his fruits, ruling and oppressing with so much violence and strength, approaches from Heaven only as Pharaoh, yet Job ... is indeed pious by not having faith. Except faith in an exodus, and faith that the last word has not yet been humanely spoken on the blood avenger, the blood-stauncher, in short, on the Son of Man ... instead of the grand master. A Word out of which one does no longer flee, but which itself, altogether without terror, enters into the sublated Above" (A, 165–66).

"The despotic might of the idea of Yahweh is eradicated in it, but what is thought of as the God of Exodus becomes effective as godless, as the Son of Man. As a highly incomplete effectivity, it is in itself by no means solved" (A, 206). Bloch leaves hardly any doubt here, though he does not diminish the fundamental importance of "Jesus' stake in Yahweh" (A, 173). And the title of Son of Man, towering over all others, is especially significant: because "the Son of Man as a pre-existent heavenly being" does "not take part in the creation of the world"; "because [this] must be the activity only at the end of time, when a new heaven and a new earth are created" (A, 209).

Clearly this is once again Bloch the Marcionite speaking, to whom we now must turn. For him, who was himself a philosopher of the religion of Exodus, the strongly inspiring and highly controversial arch-heretic Marcion[40] counts as "the most extreme" Exodus-theologian (A, 240), and he does so precisely because he denies the law-giving God of Exodus no less than he denies the creator-God of Genesis. Against the latter Marcion opposes Christ Jesus dualistically as the Savior- and Redeemer-God (A, 61): "Marcion ... sought to radically break Jesus away from the Jewish-Biblical dream of God." He

> not only posited Christ's message as one opposed to the Old Testament, but as absolutely other; so the break with the old here follows from the seemingly incomparable leap of the gospel into the new. The concept of the New Testament as such developed and was made to stand out in this form, though Marcion of course, sensing old wineskins everywhere, only included Paul's friend Luke and ten of Paul's surviving letters in his canon of 'new wine.' (A, 238–39)

For Marcion Paul is the absolute apostle, unlike anyone before or after; because in his understanding Paul was the first to contradict Yahweh "not as the creator of the world ... but instead as the *law-giver*. Paul put that hiatus between 'law' and 'gospel,' also between the 'morality of the law' and 'freedom,' 'justice' and 'grace,' so that Jesus should at least become unique" (A, 239). But even beyond this Marcionite resolution of the Pauline *dialectics* of law and gospel, Marcion extends the dualism between the two, which in fact he postulated first, to the creator and the redeemer god, or lets their duality, as the earlier and more fundamental duality, precede or

---

40. Besides Benjamin, Adorno, Marcuse, and Taubes, who have already been mentioned, I refer above all to Carl Schmitt (especially *Politische Theologie II: Die Legende von der Erledigung jeder Politischen Theologie* [Berlin: Duncker and Humblot, 1970]) and Hans Blumenberg (especially *Säkularisierung und Selbstbehauptung. Erweiterte und überarbeitete Neuausgabe von 'Die Legitimität der Neuzeit', erster und zweiter Teil* [Frankfurt: Suhrkamp, 1974], as well as *Arbeit am Mythos* [Frankfurt: Suhrkamp,1979]). Critical towards both Schmitt and Blumenberg: Richard Faber, *Der Prometheus-Komplex: Zur Kritik der Politotheologie Eric Voegelins und Hans Blumenbergs* (Würzburg: Königshausen & Neumann, 1984), Teil B (below as Excursus I).

rather found the dialectic. Either way the law is in effect assigned to the world's creator, who then tyrannically rules over the world, and the gospel to the "alien god" Jesus, who is the god of consolation.[41] This divine duality "sharpens"—as Bloch expresses himself—the antithesis between law and gospel that is not correctly Pauline in any case "to the point of *irreconcilability* and hence also the radical *novum*," which is how Marcion distinguishes the Gospel from the Old Testament (A, 239).

Intriguingly he synonymizes the radical nature of the gospel's novelty with "foreignness" and also calls the redeeming god of the gospel "alien." This god "does not call us home from foreign lands where we have gotten lost, but from the horrific home to which we belong, into a blessed foreign land."[42] This is not Bloch's, but rather the formulation of the historical theologian Adolf von Harnack in his seminal work on Marcion's *Gospel of the Alien God*. But he does so in exactly the same sense as Bloch (perhaps inspired by him[43]). As late as in his *Atheism*, for instance, Bloch speaks of "something which shines into everyone's childhood, but where no one has ever been: home" (A, 294)—as he already had done in the *Principle of Hope*, where he seems to be "orchestrating"[44] Harnack.

Certainly a problem for Bloch's understanding of Marcion is this extreme ascetic's escape from the world, even enmity towards it. The problem is that the message of this most extreme theologian of the exodus, because he leads out of *all* worldliness, is, in Bloch's understanding, "itself dark."

> For it not only leads out of captivity, like the great archetype of the exodus in the Old Testament excluded by Marcion, but out of the flesh and out of every temporality, and not into a better one. This purely pneumatic, purely *logos*–mythical farewell to the world in its asceticism sees no land before itself, one where—at least comparatively—milk and honey flow. And according to this purely pneumatic docetism of the Marcionites it became even less true that Christ had risen in flesh. Indeed the true Christ was not even born in flesh for them; thus flawed, the message of the wholly new, wholly alien god according to Marcion could not have given an impulse of such purity. Meanwhile, also here, also in this abstract asceticism so often trivialized, also with this flipside of a

---

41. Cf. Carsten Colpe, "'Das eschatologische Widerlager der Politik.' Zu Jacob Taubes's Gnosisbild," in *Abendländische Eschatologie*, edited by Faber et al., 124.

42. Harnack, *Marcion*, 225.

43. Cf. Bloch, *Geist der Utopie* (Munich: Duncker & Humblot, 1918).

44. Cf. Taubes, "Das stählerne Gehäuse und der Exodus daraus," 11.

total orientation towards the alien in Marcion's god, there is no evidence of a turn away from the human being in this world.

Bloch is convinced: "on the contrary: what was envisioned was an even more complete turn towards the human being. Towards his own, specifically designated transcendence into the foreignness of a home that is singularly identical with him" (A, 240).

Well, this is already a further developed, a "modern,"[45] a *Blochian* Marcion we are introduced to here. But this atheist philosopher, or rather this philosophical atheist, *always* thinks further and beyond both humanism and the Enlightenment. *In doing so* he recurs, in order to transcend the historical Enlightenment, to the pre-Enlightened, the religious, though always the potentially utopian. Bloch is always concerned with what will be better in the future; in that regard, one can and even should by all means polemicize against "*the existing* world," the more so when it is understood—in an apocalyptic rather than Marcionite way—as "this aeon," and when this aeon is juxtaposed with another, better one in the sense of—irony of ironies— "new *world*." There is no question that "the old one" has gone "awry"; if that was not the case, "there would be no need for a messiah" (A, 173). But there is a need for one, even if it is a fully human, indeed collective messiah: in every sense *human-some* (A, 183), and in that regard of course also containing *world*, and world-*capable*.

There is a need for rebels and revolutionaries who can and should learn from the heretics spearheaded by Marcion. Speaking only in a historical sense, Harnack—a right-wing rather than left-wing liberal—stated what I repeat here: that Tolstoy is

> a Marcionite Christian through and through. The directly religious passages we have from Marcion could well have been written by him, and conversely Marcion would have recognized himself in Tolstoy's "miserable and despised," in his reading of the Sermon on the Mount . . . and in his zeal against common Christendom. On the other hand, Gorky's moving play *The Lower Depths* can be understood as a Marcionite play as well; 'The Stranger' who appears here is the Marcionite Christ, and his 'Lower Depths' are the world.[46]

No doubt what is meant is the miserable *social* world.

---

45. Once again I refer to Taubes, "Walter Benjamin—ein moderner Marcionit?"
46. Harnack, *Marcion*, 232.

In Bloch's view it should be "blown up" by way of revolution (A, 148); here he is commemorating Marcion and certainly also thinking *normatively*. With reference to abrupt, immediate novelty he writes: "Jesus' birth ... took place in the year zero." And:

> Interpreted in a *Marcionite* way, the year zero ... is completely different from the calendar beginnings set within history, which hence merely occur, such as the Roman *ab urbe condita*. Paradoxically one could only recall the new beginning of the Jacobins' year zero, "likewise" intended to be total; its tearing away from the whole "Old Testament" of history as purely the fraud of dukes and clerics. But in this incomparably different, that is, religious topos, Marcion also rejects, with full *primeurs*, any possible historical mediation before his novum. (A, 241–42)

One should take note of how Bloch almost didactically draws an analogy, which is our sole concern here: he explicitly compares the "incomparably" different only in view of *the same* understanding of time as a radical break, the sudden and strict separation of the old and the new. Precisely with that aim, he can then *analogically* call the year of Jesus' birth "year zero" (following the example of the French Revolution) and the *ancien régime* (following the example of the "Old Covenant") "Old Testament." In a kind of circular argument, this is about the immanentization of Jewish-Christian, specifically *Marcionite* topoi after they have already been re-interpreted or rather "charged" with immanent and *social-revolutionary* meaning.

Before we turn to this in more detail, Bloch's second most important premise—after "Only an atheist can be a good Christian, only a Christian can be a good atheist"—shall be explained: "The best thing about religion is that it creates heretics" (A, 15).

6. ATHEISM IN HERETICAL CHRISTIANITY AND CHRISTIANITY IN REVISED MARXISM

The "Religion of the Exodus and the Kingdom" is judged positively by Bloch, who always understands it as heretical. Even where, and especially when it speaks biblically, it stands as a whole on the shoulders of heretics. For Bloch the authentic Bible itself is "heretical" (in a certain sense he here spells out the incredibly influential and repeatedly praised "left pietist"

Gottfried Arnold[47]). At any rate, it is "necessary to read the Bible analytically, indeed like a detective, *sub specie* of its continuing history of heresy" (A, 23). And this gets easier as biblical history often goes "against its own grain" (A, 24). Hence, what "the ruling clerics have done to it"—for example de-emphasizing the prophets in favor of the clerics (A, 101)—"in large parts" could "be corrected by beginning from Scripture" (A, 53) It is never linear, but rather contains "*contrary* principles," such as (and most importantly) creation and apocalypse, with two deeply *contradictory* basic formulas: "And behold, it was very good" and "Behold, I make all things new" (A, 59).

In short, there are—not least because of the prophetic-apocalyptic writings—possibilities for critique through the Bible (A, 111). Bloch even considers it "the most revolutionary religious book of them all" (A, 104). "There is an incisive, often repressed revolt in it against pressure, spearheaded by the unprecedented *expectation* of a truly Altogether Different which will one day fill the *earth*" (A, 111). Where it represents "the true *Biblia pauperum*"—even as a "subterranean Bible"—it intends (which is almost Marxian) the "abolition of all conditions in which the human merely lives as an oppressed, despicable, missing creature" (A, 110).

Marxism, so one of Bloch's most basic convictions,

> implies the subversive and non-static inheritance . . . that goes around . . . in the Bible. As a sublation of the whole Above in which the human does not appear, as at once a transcending with a revolt and a revolt with a transcending—even without transcendence. This is in so far as the Bible can now, at last, be read with the eyes of the Communist Manifesto, and *at the same time* can prevent all that atheist salt from losing its saltiness,[48] a salt that understands what is implicit in Marxism, using that same Meta that prevents that salt itself from losing its saltiness. (A, 98)

It goes without saying that this last point presupposes a good bit of revision of Marxism-Leninism, or is a consequence of it—and the leaders of the SED[49] understood this very well.[50] Its atheist salt, on the verge of

---

47. Cf. amongst others Leutzsch, "Das Jesusbild von Ernst Bloch," 21.

48. *Translators' note: see Mark 9:50.

49. *Translators' note: Sozialistische Einheitspartei Deutschlands.

50. I shall just hint at *Ernst Blochs Leipziger Jahre*, edited by Manfred Neuhaus and Helmut Seidel (Schkeuditz: GNN Verlag, 2001), as well as *Hoffnung kann enttäuscht werden: Ernst Bloch in Leipzig*, introd. and commentated by Volker Caysa et al. (Meisenheim/Glan: Hain, 1992).

losing its saltiness, indeed having lost it for quite some time, was meant to return to strength and saltiness, perhaps stronger and saltier than ever before. Indeed, which Marxist before Bloch would have insisted so strongly on the "unsettled" in biblical religion, and therefore would have taken "the real Christianity" seriously in a comparable way, and so being the only "real Marxist" (A, 353)? Certainly, for his part the young Marx had no reductive understanding of Christianity, and hence he is Bloch's shibboleth against all later and contemporary reductionism (A, 352). He is fully right to point out the complete isolation of the famous-infamous sentence about religion as "the opium of the people" and is keen on its firm recontextualization: "this very true sentence on the opium of the people stands in an equally true and at the same time much more profound context than the vulgar materialists would like and can bear it to be," writes Bloch, to introduce his extended quotation from Marx:

> Religion is the fantastic realization of the human being, since the human being has not acquired any true reality.... Religious suffering is at once the expression of real suffering and at the same time a protest against real suffering. Religion is the sigh of the oppressed creature, the heart of a heartless world, and the soul of soulless conditions. It is the opium of the people. The sublation of religion as the illusory happiness of the people is the demand for their real happiness.... Criticism has plucked the imaginary flowers on the chain not in order that man shall continue to bear that chain without fantasy or consolation, but so that he shall throw off the chain and pluck the living flower.... The criticism of religion ends with the teaching that man is the highest creature for man—hence, with the categorical imperative to overthrow all relations in which man is a debased, enslaved, abandoned, despicable creature. (A, 91–92)

"So only in this way," comments Bloch, "the context becomes complete, including a 'sigh', even 'protest' against the current bad conditions, and audibly it cries not for sedation alone. Against all vulgarization it signifies (amongst other things), that the sermon in the German Peasant War was indeed more than and different from a 'religious cover,' as Kautsky later thought" (A, 92). Throughout his life Bloch could not stop worrying that the "Enlightenment ... should be perfected" not only against "shoddy superstition," "but unfortunately, against vulgar Marxism, and against the thundering prophets, against those so-called 'little bits of apocalyptic mysticism,' the taste of which not even Kautsky liked in Thomas Münzer" (A, 19–20).

Quite different is the response of Bloch's friend Bertold Brecht, who—like Kautsky and of course Bloch himself—"hated popish obfuscation to the point of retching." But nonetheless, when asked about his favorite reading material, he replied: "'You're probably going to laugh: the Bible.' As cheeky and surprising as this was, it was surprising only for the kind of educated people that never go away, and who confuse Enlightenment with En-*litterment*[51]" (A, 20). Indeed, this comment demonstrates that Bloch was fighting against (a) clericalism as much as what he called "En-litterment."[52] He formulates his very concrete and *synthesized* utopia as follows: "Just as a non-banal movement of the godless always could and will read the Bible, so will a subterranean, paradoxical, biblical heresy read the movement of the godless—to the benefit of both. The former gains depth ('banality,' Isaac Babel said, 'is the counter-revolution'), while the latter gains a Promethean-active, atheist-utopian understanding [*Verstand*] of human becoming" (A, 22).

7. META-ENLIGHTENMENT

I cannot elaborate here on the deeply moving words Bloch wrote on "the Bible of *humanity*,"[53] which is much more than "the most important work of world literature"[54]—though it is indeed that, too. Yet I have to emphasize that he wrote all that under the the principled and emphatic imputation of biblical criticism; it was one of "the most exciting examples of human

---

51. *Translators' note: Bloch's word-creation *Aufkläricht* combines *Aufklärung* (Enlightement) with *Kehricht* (litter, rubbish).

52. Horst Folkers has very well summarized: "As a reader of the Bible Bloch tries to please no one, not the Marxists and the Enlightened contemporaries, because he reads the Bible with such intensity and impartiality as if the truth was immediately written down there; not the Jews, because he reads the New Testament with the same naturalness as he reads the Old Testament and finds in it . . . the solution to the question of Job; finally not the Christians, because he reads the Bible of the Old and New Testament as an integral Jewish book and wants to hear nothing about the church" (Folkers, "Transzendenz und Utopie in Ernst Bloch's 'Atheismus im Christentum.'" In *Vom Jenseits. Jüdisches Denken in der europäischen Geistesgeschichte*, edited by Eveline Goodman–Thau [Berlin: Akademie-Verlag, 1997], 111).

53. Ernst Bloch, *Leipziger Vorlesungen zur Geschichte der Philosophie*, vol. 1 (Frankfurt: Suhrkamp, 1985), 491.

54. Cf. Jan Milič Lochman, "Eine atheistische Interpretation der Bibel," *Reformatio* 20 (1972), 232.

acuity" (A, 104). Nonetheless, it should also become a *saving* criticism[55] in the way he exercises it, uniting itself with the criticism contained in the Bible itself, and hence in a manner superior to the "trivial" enlightenment. Bloch has no problem with so-called secularization, only it must not be "dull" (H, 1521).

He is vehemently *in favor of* profanization, and *agreeingly* he cites Friedrich Engels: "Before the existing social conditions could be attacked, they had to be stripped of their halo of sanctity" (H, 1528). Still, even Engel's definition of materialism, which he shares in principle, finds Bloch's assent: "the explanation of the world through itself," and connected to this of course the rejection of "a heaven above, with a God as master: his case was closed not only scientifically, but by the critique of ideology he was filed away under 'pre-history,' which lasts until today, as he himself legitimized, *sanctified* the master-slave relation, the social heteronomy on earth. This way the subversive gets the last word against everything heteronomous, but also against the most useful illusion: the theocratic (from way above)," as Bloch approvingly recognizes. Still, he could hardly applaud the fact that for many "the role, the topos of religion" seemed "to be fully exhausted" (A, 20). He synthesizes—in his idiolect—the "warm and the cold current" in Marxism: "To see through history and its ideologies like a detective is part of... the cold current in Marxist thought, but the purpose that is sought, the distant, human-oriented goal of this seeing-through, is part of... the warm current of original Marxism, indeed undeniably it is part of the first, Christ-formed basic text on the 'Kingdom of Freedom'" (A, 349–50). Moreover, which is not surprising in the least: both currents are meritorious and necessary. Or rather: one current is the *corrective* of the other.

Sub specie Marxism(-Leninism)—it is well known that Marx did not want to be "a Marxist"—the utopia that Engels prematurely considered overcome is to be revitalized, and within its frame, indeed as its Wherefrom and its Where-to, the "religion of Exodus and the Kingdom" must be revitalized as well. Or, to epitomize further: (Marxist) atheism has to be *Christianized* in a dialectical manner, whereby "dialectical" means not least that such a Christianization does not negate atheism, but rather *presupposes* it. Bloch's concern is *Christianity* in atheism, but only because he always

---

55. On the concept of "saving criticism," see not least Peter Bürger, "Benjamins 'rettende Kritik.' Vorüberlegungen zum Entwurf einer kritischen Hermeneutik," *Germ.-Rom. Monatsschr.* N.F. 23 (1973), 198ff.

already starts from "Atheism *in* Christianity": "Only an atheist can be a good Christian, only a Christian can be a good atheist" (A, 15).

We shall leave behind now the first part of the sentence by translating it into the final result: good Christianity presupposes the enlightenment, which includes atheism. Yet, once again: Why does the good atheist also have to be a Christian? Because, as Bloch first answers negatively,

> triviality becomes the pathetic, nihilism the hellish effect . . . once the disenchantment of transcendence has also dispelled every well-founded *transcendere*, a utopia well founded in the content of man and world. Fear may be removed by triviality, but at the price of a different narrowness: atrophy. In nihilism fear is also removed, but at an even higher price: despair. However, a *concrete* disenchantment leads not into triviality, but a shock about what has never before entered a human's mind and gaze, that is, what lies in the Not-Yet-Become; and it leads not into nihilism, but the well-founded hope that it is not the last word. (A, 316)

"Real Enlightenment neither trivializes nor destroys the background" (A, 313), as Bloch's relevant chapter heading aphoristically decrees. But we shall first explain the hellish effect of nihilism—with Bloch and the best example of all:

> New paganism . . . , also drawing on Haeckel and Bölsche, as well as on "The forest is my Church," by no means abolished true slave morality and even less the masters' press. Where the law of the fittest, including their natural selection, replaced the sermon of love, it became clear . . . that not every abolition of the Bible may be Enlightenment, that Nero's torches may burn even more brightly. But in addition to these fruits: the Enlightened educated Philistine from long ago, from before Haeckel, Bölsche and the forest as church—he showed that not only faith is blinding. "The Truth about Monasteries and the Stupidification of the People," also "Moses or Darwin?"—these little tracts by the half-educated, and hence the only half-disenchanted, did not make the thought of the so-called freethinker in those days any lighter or more capacious. But above all, this remains instructive: in a world that had become anti-Biblical, jumping across Yuletide fires became particularly easy, because it is not from Jesse's lineage. There was also no clear support for conscience, even in a clerical and therefore still spiritual movement. Against the holy spring of German power, especially when it was thought to be flowing so clearly from the Antichrist. If it had been Francis of Assisi instead of the whore

of Babylon in the background, it would have had a much harder time. (A, 40–41)

Perhaps Bloch is too kind at the end—in clerical-fascist Croatia, Franciscans were the "avant garde" of the pogrom—but there is no doubt about what he formulates elsewhere in this way:

> Certainly nihilism . . . also has . . . premises in mechanical materialism; it has them in the cosmological pointlessness and aimlessness. As mere circulation of moving matter, existence has no meaning: in this absolutized disenchantment, existence has gone completely to the dogs, the apes, the atoms. In contrast, apart from physical-chemical starting points, dialectical materialism (with the sign above its gate: no mechanist shall enter here) knows a continuous series of starting points, hot spots of production: the cell, economic man, the arch-qualitative interlacings of base and superstructure . . . Most importantly, it knows the really existing *problem* of a human-qualified Kingdom of Freedom: all antidotes to triviality and nihilism, or the activation of what is precisely not the opium, or even the pressing idol of religion. (A, 316)

It is precisely

> after all the opium and the fools' paradise of the afterlife have burnt down . . . [that] the secret appears which is adequate to the undaunted human being. Precisely the affect assigned to this secret and so alien to triviality and nihilism—reverence—represents the reception of something uncanny without any fear, of something monstrous without inhumanity. Reverence has as a correlate that sublimity which transports an intimation of our future freedom. It signifies a *transcendere* without any self-alienation at all, and as a correlate of this surmounting, this outdoing it does not signify the hypostasis of a frightful idol, but the latency of our intended day of rising, in which neither fear nor ignorance has a refuge, but instead the wish to know and the ability to know hope find their source. *The Messianic is the red secret of every revolutionary Enlightenment that sustains itself in plenitude.*"[Bloch's italics.] (A, 317)

Some pages down he repeats in different words: "Everywhere the Messianic is the last support of life, but also at the same time the last thing from the utopian truth shining in," *and he adds*: "For the all too wise, this is foolishness; the all too pious turn it into a pre-fabricated house, (but) for the wise the utopian meaning is the most solid, really existing problem of the world itself, the unsolved world. And in this way life has as much meaning as develops first in discontent, work, the fissure of what is inadequate for us, intuition of the measured; surmounting, not eccentric" (A, 334–35). Or to use another one of Bloch's favorite idioms: Full of hope, but without any confidence, or even guarantee.

8. UTOPIAN AND MILITANT THIS-WORLDLINESS

For Bloch a belief in a heavenly beyond always seemed outrageously eccentric and the epitome of all "reified confidence" (A, 324). Such fundamentalism for him was worth fighting against, just as it was worth fighting the belief in a hypostasized, equally otherworldly God. Indeed, with Feuerbach, he is in favor of a "de-heavening" (A, 281) in all respects, of course in order to—as the young Hegel already formulated—"vindicate the treasures squandered to heaven as the property of humanity" (A, 95). Supernatural transcendence is rejected, but inner-natural *transcending* is explicitly demanded (A, 282): "A transcending without transcendence" (A, 15), but certainly with an *eschatological* telos. Fully turned inwards to the anthropological, the innerworldly *utopian*, Bloch over and over again proclaims with Augustine against Augustine: "*Dies septimus nos ipsi erimus*" (A, 15).

"Atheism is the premise of *concrete* utopia, but a concrete utopia is the equally indispensable implication of atheism. Atheism with a concrete utopia is, via one and the same thorough act, the obliteration of religion as well as the *heretical* hope of religion put on its human feet" (A, 317). Once again this means that Christian religion of a heretical kind is the irreplacable reservoir and potential of every utopianism, especially since no heavenly hope, but certainly a worldly hope, was widely at work in Judaism and broadly in Christianity *itself*: the "unprecedented expectation of a truly Altogether-Different, which will one day fill the *earth*," (A, 111) as Bloch formulated.

The story of creation has always been read as an (also) eschatological one.[56] In any case, Bloch comments specifically on the para-biblical myth of the Makanthropos "*Adam* Kadmon" as follows: "The image of the form here is an *image of the aim*; under Adam Kadmon only Alpha and Omega

---

56. Cf. Richard Faber, "'Mit uns zieht die neue Zeit.' Differenzierungen in der Kategorie 'Novum,'" in *Säkularisierung und Resakralisierung. Zur Geschichte des Kirchenlieds und seiner Rezeption*, edited by Faber (Würzburg: Königshausen & Neumann, 2001), 189–97, especially 193–95.

were seriously considered, and the Alpha only just so the Omega of the *end* would be in sight throughout the whole creation. Makanthropos is the head at the end of the world, the shape of the future *kingdom*. In this sense, the weighty humanism of such a vision justifiably survived in Christian speculation, no longer in a cosmocentric sense, but one that put its faith in *humans*" (A, 203).

Of course, Marcion's preaching of the alien end-god, which still touches on the Makanthropos myth, is to be "hominized," as Bloch frankly admits, whilst still holding on to its utopian essence: "The Son of Man Christ (Jesus) surely has no god, that is also no alien god, above himself . . ., but then Marcion's phantasm had its High-above only as a signalling light towards us from Atopos," (A, 243) or rather *Outopos*.

This is Bloch's projection hypothesis in this specific case, vindicating a High–above to something futuric or, as it were, *utopian*. As regards Exodus, prophecy, and apocalypticism, he only needs to continue re-writing in a social-revolutionary manner, to re-write what was already then an inner-worldly—increasingly eschatological—promise. "Even just to be able to sit under a vine without anyone making one afraid becomes [in the prophets] a future, as well as the land where milk and honey were meant to flow, as well as a justice of Yahweh that would fill the earth and the sea (Isa 48:18)"[57] (A, 143). The salvific image of the heavenly Jerusalem as a new heaven and a new earth in John's Revelation was also meant to signify a re-creation [*Umschaffung*] of this *immanent* world. The city of Jerusalem is a proper new heaven only in so far as it has a real qualitative alterity as opposed to the old *aeon*. This means that the blissful alterity of heaven is essential for the heavenly Jerusalem. Yet heaven is not conceived as God's private space, but instead as a *city of humans*, cleared of all images of the divine that existed up until now, a city which is built according to the measurements of the Son of Man, who is not only the authoritative architectural principle of this city, but at once its inner and innermost steering principle.[58]

"The inhabitants of this new Jerusalem will be citizens of a human existence that has finally come to consciousness," concludes Elke Kruttschnitt, Bloch's interpreter, speaking as a *social* philosopher.[59] Earlier, the Marxist Bloch himself had put a communist emphasis on the social dimension of the "Kingdom of God" as man's final destination: ". . . the Philadelphia of a

---

57. *Translators' note: see Mic 4:4.
58. Cf. Kruttschnitt in Faber, "'Mit uns zieht die neue Zeit,'" 196.
59. Ibid.

Atheism in Christianity—Christianity in Atheism

communism of love is the basic premise of the Kingdom; and in this way it becomes a worldly norm," (A, 187) as Bloch emphasizes. His utopia is a *social* utopia, and quite essentially so, indeed in an active, even *militant* way:

> Optimism is justified only as militant, never as complete; in light of the world's misery in this last form it is not merely wicked, but actually imbecilic (*Das Prinzip Hoffnung*, 1624). Equally: in its concrete form, utopia is the will to the being of the All, a will that has undergone trial; in utopia, the suffering of being is at work, which had previously turned towards an order of the world supposedly already founded and successful, even a kind of overworld order [Überweltordnung]. Yet this suffering is only effective inasmuch as it belongs to the Not-Yet-Being, and to the hope for the *summum bonum* in it. Moreover, after the use of that nothingness in which history still continues, this suffering does not look away from the danger of extinction, not even from the hypothetical possibility of Nothingness as the definite end. What counts here instead is the *work* of militant optimism: in the same way that the proletariat and the bourgeoisie may sink into the same barbarity without it, so without this work, deeper down and further on, there may still be the threat of a sea without a shore, of a midnight without a sunrise, as the final state of things. This kind of finality would then signify the absolute futility of the historical process; and as something that has not yet happened, it can be no less excluded as a possibility than, in a positive sense, the finality of an All filling all. So finally there is the changeable alternative between an absolute Nothing and an absolute All: the absolute Nothing is the sealed thwarting of utopia; the absolute All—in the pre-appearance of the Kingdom of Freedom—is the sealed fulfilment of utopia or Being like utopia (loc. cit., 364). (A, 326–27)

I shall explain this Blochian self-collage as follows:

- The hope, not confidence, he champions is one that "connects with the indignation which is grounded in the concrete given possibilities of a new existence, as a salvation in the future in a trial that is by no means already thwarted, though neither is it already won" (A, 165).

- Particularly in the Bible, and there from the very beginning, "the last word about what one should do, and what is done to oneself, has not yet been said" (A, 58).

Political Demonology

- Above all, "the land of wish and will in biblical prophecy" can be discerned through a "changeable fate as anti-fate" (A, 139).[60] As it says with realism and expressionism in Bloch's earlier hagiography of Thomas Münzer, this also means that: "Here there is no guaranteed path to salvation from high above, 'but a harsh, dangerous voyage, suffering, wandering, erring, searching for the hidden home; full of tragic disturbance throughout, boiling, split with cracks, outbreaks, lonely promises, (only) discontinuously charged with the conscience of light.' (*Thomas Münzer als Theologe der Revolution*, 1962, p. 14)" (A, 325).

9. THE OPTIMISM OF A REALIST

That Bloch rejected what he called "materialized despair" no less than he rejected "materialized confidence" will not surprise anyone. However, his vehement protest against any "trivialization of the negative" (A, 324) is perhaps underappreciated.[61]

I shall bring to mind again something Bloch felt was problematic: "since the Enlightenment (i.e., since the revolution passed its decree against the devouring, the evil, the fiendish), the so-called satanic..., much more than the theistic," may not have gone out of "literarily exciting fashion," but it is no longer a "concept subject to philosophically enlightening reflection." "To enlighten here means," as Bloch is quite certain, "not so much to denounce with the aim of making visible that which is against the light, so that in all its appearances it may be centrally displayed, stated, and made contestable. [Instead,] in the optimism of the Enlightenment... evil is to be ... regarded as merely weak and small, like mere blemishes on an otherwise perfect world. But precisely for the battle, for the sake of its most thorough target"—in Bloch's view—

> more concepts such as delusion, the aggressive drive, and so on, on the *subjective* side, and all inhumanities of the class-like mode of production and exchange, all the oppressions and wars on the

---

60. Extensively: Klaus Heinrich, *Parmenides und Jona* (Basel: Stroemfeld, 1982), as well as Jürgen Ebach, *Kassandra und Jona. Gegen die Macht des Schicksals* (Frankfurt: Athenäum, 1987).

61. Even by Günther Anders; cf. Faber, "*Sagen lassen sich die Menschen nichts, aber erzählen lassen sie sich alles.*" Über Grimm–Hebelsche Erzählung, Moral und Utopie in Benjaminscher Perspektive (Würzburg: Königshausen & Neumann, 2002), 119–30.

Atheism in Christianity—Christianity in Atheism

social-*objective* side . . . are nonetheless insufficient to causally explain a phenomenon like Auschwitz, or even just to put it into representative yet non-reductive language of experience. Even Schopenhauer, the only philosopher of the nineteenth century who set out to describe his "thing in itself," the will to life, as a creature of the devil, in his description of the horrific night that his world-as-will is plunged into, never consistently reached the speaking speechlessness of that horror, which only Dante has pointed at in the *Lasciate ogni speranza* on the gate . . . [of the] *Inferno*. (A, 319–20)

Bloch's realism, or rather his materialism, is so realistic that he fully factors in Kant's "radical evil" and hence dismisses not even hell and the devil as merely horrific *fairy tales*.[62] For Bloch, Christianity and Judaism are to be taken very seriously, in large part because they—before Kant and after him—know the *topoi* of hell and the devil. Bloch's Christianity in atheism, as the counterpart to his explicitly declared atheism in Christianity—integral as it is—is also Satanism in atheism. In any case, he clearly distances himself from the kind of atheism that declares that everything satanic, no less than everything divine, is beyond discussion, not even in discussions of myth. Bloch is almost horrified that "the shallow-optimistic denial of evil in the world, this Enlightenment taking the easy way out of it" finds "a refuge" in such an atheism (A, 324).

His atheism is one that is enlightened also about the Enlightenment—enlightened in large part by Christianity. Atheism means meta-enlightenment, particularly so *in religionibus,* but at the same time, and here I quote Bloch word for word, it means "*meta-religious* humanism" (H, 1521) after Feuerbach has already "broken up the triviality of Enlitterment. . . ," and he did so "through the power of the human" (H, 1521). But *Bloch's* "anthropological atheism" goes beyond those long-outdated Left Hegelians, because his reintegration of heaven into human subjectivity implies not a static but a utopian concept of the human being. So the heart of the matter is still an anthropological re-duction; but the utopian human being, by virtue of a concept adequate to him, is given such divine depth and heavenly otherness that Bloch's reduction can no longer be misunderstood as reductionism.[63]

---

62. Cf. once again: Faber, "*Sagen lassen sich die Menschen nichts,*" in particular 107ff.; as regards Kant's and others' "radical evil," I refer to Christoph Schulte, *Die Karriere des Bösen: Kants radikales Böses und seine Wirkungsgeschichte in der ersten Hälfte des 19. Jahrhunderts* (Munich: Fink, 1988).

63. Cf. E. Kruttschnitt, in Faber, "*Sagen lassen sich die Menschen nichts,*" 372.

Political Demonology

Already "the growing humanization of religion [within itself] by no means . . . corresponds to a relaxation of its horrors. On the contrary: the *humanum* in addition now gains the mystery of a divine, of something that can be deified" (H, 1409). However, "only to the *deus absconditus* adheres the *question* of what the legitimate mystery of the *homo absconditus* is all about" (H, 1406). The *"anthropos agnostos"* (A, 200) remains a mystery, but it is a, if not the, philosophically legitimate one.

Bloch's anthropological atheism begins with the words *"Deus homo factus est,"* but because for him it is all about "the final biblical turn of events, the biblical Exodus out of Yahweh" (A, 212), he remains anthropological, exceeding even the moral [*sittlich*] atheism of Job and the prophets (A, 163). As it is also a *socialist* atheism, it accepts that heritage. At the same time, at once and once again, Bloch's atheism surmounts Feuerbach's *individual* humanism. One theological consequence, or rather, a premise of this is the reception of the Kingdom–topos, which is now *social*-anthropological: the Kingdom-*utopia*, "the humanum gains the mystery of a divine, of something that can be deified . . . as the future formation of the Kingdom" (H, 1409). Indeed,

> God *becomes* the Kingdom of God, and the Kingdom of God *no longer* has a God in it. That is: this religious heteronomy and its materialized hypostasis fully dissolves into the theology of the community, but as one that itself has crossed the threshold of the creature hitherto, its anthropology and sociology. Precisely for this reason, the very religion that proclaimed the Kingdom of God to be in our midst (cf. Luke 17:21) has most decisively held up the Wholly Other against the old Adam and the old createdness as it has come down to us. Here as a rebirth, there as a new heaven and a new earth, as the transfiguration of nature. It is this *borderline content* of the wonderful, that is: the totally redeemed, which nonetheless turns the best human society into a means to an end, the end of the totally redeemed, which has been religiously thought of as lying within the Kingdom. And whose unattainability may be discerned even in the best of all societies: as the unsublated frailty of the creature, the unsublated immediacy of the surrounding nature—a borderline content which, as a consequence, also opposes every partial optimism of several social utopias that have fallen out of the *totum of utopia*. (H, 1408)

In his *Atheism* book Bloch goes so far as to declare that Marxism has "plenty in common with Christianity and its transition to the religion of the

Roman state" (A, 315). But be that as it may: socialism, or rather communism, is no end in itself, even though it is an absolutely necessary means—of course not even a sufficient one—to that end: what is religiously conceived as the "Kingdom." This end is, if at first theologically, *hypostasized* as God personally, himself not a "Nothing"; this he would only be "if atheism were nihilism, not only of theoretical hopelessness, but a nihilism that universally and materially destroys every substantial possibility of a final end and perfection" (H, 1412). But since, as of now, this is not the case, the *principle of hope* is in effect (until further notice); it *lacks* principle in so far as this hope presents itself without guarantee, indeed without confidence. But of course precisely in this way it converges with a "militant optimism."

As Lucien Goldmann has pointed out, Bloch's hope shares some features with Pascal's Wager on the existence of God. The certainty of that hope is also an "absolute, absolutely uncertain certainty."[64] To quote Bloch himself: "Nothing and Everything, Chaos and Kingdom are lying on the scales in the former area of religious projection; and it is the human labor in history that weighs heavily on the side of the Everything or Nothing" (H, 1532). Yet because of this, once the bet has been made—and one cannot evade it, only decide in favor of the nothing (if that is a decision at all)—then all objective reasons are consulted in order to increase the (Pascalian) faith that is the basis of this bet. Similarly the (Blochian) hope is taught and is itself being taught, whereby it justifies its doings and its doings in return justify this hope itself.

It goes without saying that in the end *action* has to be taken; it all depends on the "human *labor* in history"—Bloch could only laugh (or cry) about all historical automatisms. Hence there is no way to forego the (Marxist-inspired) *social revolution*. For this world-revolutionary it has by no means primacy, but at all times it has priority, the dialectical relationship of which Bloch has expressed in an "Haggadian" way or "parabolically"[65] through this Chassidim story:

"It is as the Baalshem says: the Messiah can only come when all the guests have sat down at the table; but it is first and foremost the table of labor and only after that the table of the Lord. In the secret of the Kingdom,

---

64. Lucien Goldmann, *Weltflucht und Politik: Dialektische Studien zu Pascal und Racine* (Neuwied a. Rh.; Berlin: Luchterhand, 1967), 99.

65. On the notion of *aggada*, cf. Chaim N. Bialik, "Halacha und Aggada." In: Bialik, *Drei Essays* (Berlin: 1925), 82–107, as well as Faber, "*Sagen lassen sich die Menschen nichts,*" especially Chapter 4.

the organization of the world has its immediately effective, its immediately deductive metaphysics."[66]

---

66. Bloch, *Geist der Utopie*, 411.

III

Political Demonology
On the Counter-Revolutionary Marcionism of Carl Schmitt and Others

> One doesn't fight for something, but against something:
> Hatred is the dominant note of war, not love.
>
> —Helmuth James Graf von Moltke,
> in a letter dated November 8, 1942

INTRODUCTION

The subtitle of my third part is also indebted to Jacob Taubes's explicit enquiry of Gershom Scholem: "Walter Benjamin—a Modern Marcionite?"[1] Yet in terms of subject matter, the decisive "reference person" for the title and subtitle is Carl Schmitt (who was for Taubes, after Benjamin and Scholem, almost equally important[2]):

---

1. Jacob Taubes, in *Antike und Moderne: Zu Walter Benjamins "Passagen,"* edited by Norbert W. Bolz and Richard Faber (Würzburg: Königshausen & Neumann, 1986), 138ff.

2. Cf. Jacob Taubes, *Ad Carl Schmitt: Gegenstrebige Fügung* (Berlin: Merve, 1987).

Political Demonology

- Political demonology disfigures Schmitt's talk about "political Christology"[3] back *into* recognition;

- the following quote (from *Political Theology II*) substantiates my claim that he apperceives a modern Marcionism, although the names of Benjamin and Marcion do not explicitly come up:[4]

> The structural core problem of the Gnostic dualism between the god of creation and the god of redemption governs . . . not only every religion of salvation and redemption. It is immanently given in every world in need of change and renewal, inescapably and ineradicably. . . . The lord of a world in need of change, i.e., a misconceived world—a lord to whom the need for change is ascribed, since he refuses to submit to it but instead resists it—and the liberator, the creator of a transformed, new world cannot be good friends. They are, so to speak, enemies *by definition*.[5]

Whether they are necessarily "Manichaean" enemies[6] is a question for expert historians of ancient gnosis;[7] but one should be able to, or even must, speak about a "demonization" of the enemy in question (as Schmitt does in the previous quote). But certainly it is a "total"[8] or rather "absolute" enmity: an understanding of the enemy as a "criminal," and even a "beast that has to be not just repelled, but definitely *destroyed*."[9] It is true (before 1933 as well as after 1945) that Schmitt repeatedly emphasizes that the *differentiation* between enemy and criminal was achieved with the—for him

---

3. Carl Schmitt, *Politische Theologie II. Die Legende von der Erledigung jeder politischen Theologie* (Berlin: Duncker and Humblot, 1970), 11.

4. As regards Schmitt's lively interest in Benjamin, see, besides his *Hamlet und Hekuba* dated 1956 and *Politische Theologie II*, 116 n. 2, also Helmut Lethen, "Über das Spiel von Infamien," in *Belles lettres/Graffiti: Soziale Phantasien und Ausdrucksformen der Achtundsechziger*, edited by Ulrich Ott and Roman Luckscheiter (Göttingen: Wallstein-Verlag, 2001), 53–66.

5. Schmitt, *Politische Theologie II*, 120–21.

6. Ibid., 119.

7. Cf. Guy Stroumsa, "König und Schwein: Zur Struktur des manichäischen Dualismus," in *Gnosis und Politik*, edited by Jacob Taubes (Paderborn: F. Schöningh, 1984), 141–53.

8. Cf. above all Carl Schmitt, "Totaler Feind, totaler Krieg, totaler Staat" (1937), in Schmitt, *Positionen und Begriffe im Kampf mit Weimar—Genf—Versailles 1923-1939* (Hamburg: Hanseatische Verlagsanstalt, 1940), 236.

9. Carl Schmitt, *Der Begriff des Politischen. Text von 1932 mit einem Vorwort und drei Corollarien* (Berlin: Duncker and Humblot, 1963), 17, 37.

"classical"—"*Jus Publicum Europaeum*," spearheaded by Thomas Hobbes.[10] But still he always has to admit and equally emphasize

1. that the non-criminalizing, not even "discriminating" concept of the enemy (in the form of "cabinet wars")[11] was applied only to *European* peoples (or rather states);[12]

2. that as a result of World War I the age of sovereign nations or rather "states" has drawn to a close, and so the *Jus Publicum Europaeum* with its principle of restricted enmity and warfare has also come to an end.

As early as 1937 Schmitt establishes "total enemy, total war, total state" as *one* connection, and in the essay of the same name he expounds: "The sort and form of the state's totality defines itself from total war . . . But total war only has meaning by virtue of the total enemy."[13] It is *this* enmity that is now at stake, first and finally. The introductory sentence of *The Concept of the Political*, the treatise with which Schmitt founded his doctrine of the enemy in 1929, had read: "The concept of the state presupposes the concept of the political."[14] The other important book here, the 1970 *Political Theology II*, is *still* in line with this: "Today one can no longer define the political by beginning from the state. On the contrary, whatever one may still take to be the state must be defined and grasped by beginning from the political. Yet the criterion for the political . . . today is the degree of the intensity of association or dissociation, meaning: the distinction between friend and enemy."[15]

Especially with a view to the subject "Political Theology" (which was at first a doctrine of the state, or rather a doctrine of "sovereignty"[16]) it says ten pages earlier and quite consistently: "The thematic development of my treatise 'Political Theology' dated 1922 (2nd edition 1934, R.F.) has a general direction which . . . can be discerned everywhere today: from

---

10. Schmitt, *Politische Theologie II*, 110–11.

11. Cf. Schmitt, *Die Wendung zum diskriminierenden Kriegsbegriff*, 3rd ed. (Berlin: Duncker and Humblot, 2003).

12. Cf. Schmitt, *Der Begriff des Politischen*, 11.

13. Schmitt, "Totaler Feind," 236.

14. Schmitt, *Der Begriff des Politischen*, 20; cf. also ibid., 13; and Schmitt, *Politische Theologie II*, 25.

15. Schmitt, *Politische Theologie II*, 25.

16. Note that the subtitle of *Political Theology* (I), dated 1922 and 1934, is "Four Chapters on the Concept of Sovereignty."

political theology to political Christology."[17] Political Christology, however, *for Schmitt*[18] means a "stasiology"[19] (which he thinks must be fought), that is, a doctrine of insurrection, even civil war; hence Christology is *in essence* polemical. Nevertheless, it remains "Theology," as the synonym "Christology" already suggests. Yet Schmitt explicitly also uses the term "New political theology," making the point that in essence it is a "Political theology of the New."[20] We recall:

> The structural core problem of the Gnostic dualism between the god of creation and the god of redemption governs . . . not only every religion of salvation and redemption. It is immanently given in every world in need of change and renewal, inescapably and ineradicably . . . The lord of a world to be changed, i.e., a misconceived world . . . and the creator of a transformed, new world cannot be good friends. They are, so to speak, enemies *by definition*.[21]

Where the "counter-god" still carries the name "Antichrist"—both Schmitt and Benjamin use it[22]—he must be "overcome,"[23] and so he is an "absolute" enemy. Schmitt (though not Benjamin!) speaks in the central passage we just quoted a second time as a Gnostic, indeed as a *Marcionite*; the explanations immediately preceding our quotation leave no doubt about it: "Gnostic dualism juxtaposes the God of love, a God *alien to this world*, viewed as God of salvation, with the just God, the Lord and creator of this evil world. The two gods are in a state of open war, or at least in a relationship of unbridgeable alienation similar to a kind of dangerous Cold War, in which the enmity can be more intense than any enmity found in the naivety of a fight on traditional battlefields."[24]

---

17. Schmitt, *Politische Theologie II*, 11.

18. "Political Christology" has a different meaning in, e.g., Ernst H. Kantorowicz's *King's Two Bodies: A Study in Mediaeval Political Theology* (Princeton: Princeton University Press, 1957); cf. R. Faber, "Walter Benjamins *Ursprung des deutschen Trauerspiels* und Ernst H. Kantorowicz's *Die zwei Körper des Königs*. Ein Vergleich," in *Geschichtskörper. Zur Aktualität von Ernst H. Kantorowicz*, edited by Wolfgang Ernst and Cornelia Vismann (Munich: Fink, 1998), 171ff., esp. 179ff.

19. Schmitt, *Politische Theologie II*, 123.

20. Ibid., 35.

21. Ibid., 120–21.

22. Cf. ibid., 81.

23. Cf. Walter Benjamin, *Illuminationen. Ausgewählte Schriften* (Frankfurt: Suhrkamp, 1969), 270.

24. Schmitt, *Politische Theologie II*, 119–20; emphasis added.

Political Demonology

For the moment I will leave aside how Schmitt brings God's enmity—indeed even the gods' enmity—up to date in *contemporary* history; suffice to say that it politicizes the Yahweh-Christ opposition in principle; it even metaphysically, or rather theologically, indeed christologically *grounds* political antagonisms, not only with regard to the Cold War. Expressed in terms of the sociology of religion: at least since the "arch-heretic" Marcion, within Christianity there inheres—christologically, and hence theologically immanent—a readiness for insurrection ranging from the latent to the potential, as well as a dominant tendency for order and subjugation (at any cost). John Milton, for example, enhanced the obviously revolutionary struggle of Satan with his own revolutionary experience, making the vanquished revolutionary a Puritan, and the reactionary God a Stuart.[25] Milton drew the final possible consequence from a "political Christology" in Schmitt's sense[26]: to oppose *Satan*-Christ and God-*Father*. Pierre Joseph Proudhon will do the same, and Donoso Cortés for his part will demonize the Utopian Socialist. Whether negative or positive, Political Theology, like Political Christology, implies political *demonology*, even if Schmitt—an open partisan and successor of Cortés—would like to obscure that (with a hostile eye toward Karl Marx,[27] Ernst Bloch, and the contemporary theologians indebted to Bloch: Johann Baptist Metz and Jürgen Moltmann[28]).

1. THE COUNTER-REVOLUTIONARY APOCALYPTICISM OF DONOSO CORTÉS AND CARL SCHMITT

Let's first look at Schmitt's pivotal teacher—before Hobbes—and his illustrative dispute with Proudhon. Schmitt leaves no doubt as to his significance (especially after 1945): "With every intensification of world-historical development, from 1848 and 1918 up to the global World Civil War of the present, his [Cortés'] importance has grown along with it, and it has done so in the same way that the rescuer grows along with the danger. To fully bring this into recognition is the aim of our publication. It aims to help

---

25. Cf. Christopher Caudwell, *Bürgerliche Illusion und Wirklichkeit. Beiträge zur materialistischen Ästhetik*, trans. by Horst Bretschneider (Munich: Hanser, 1971), 82.
26. Cf. Schmitt, *Politische Theologie II*, 119.
27. Cf. Schmitt, *Der Begriff des Politischen*, 73.
28. Cf. Schmitt, *Politische Theologie II*, 31–9 and 117–18 n.3.

make sure that now, for the third time, Donoso's name is no longer left unheard and that his words unfold their power."[29]

For this purpose Schmitt sets all his hopes in Cortés' speech *sans phrase*—the famous, infamous one in favor of dictatorship, which this actively political lay-theologian regarded "as a fact of the divine order." For Cortés, God himself now and again "acts" "dictatorially," by "breaking through ... the laws" that "he himself has given to himself."[30] The point of this is of course that Cortés understands this worldly-political dictatorship mainly to be as illegal as it is illegitimate: "If legality suffices to save society, then legality—if not, then dictatorship! This horrendous word ..., though by no means as horrendous as the word revolution, the most horrendous of all words."[31] And neither constitutional nor legitimist legality *can possibly* prevent the revolution. The revolutions of 1830 (1834) and 1848 have proven this; hence Cortés brings "his decisionism to a conclusion,"[32] as Schmitt approvingly comments.

For Cortés, who now has the Revolution before his eyes, only the naked sword can be at hand. He is convinced that the moment of the final battle has come; "[yet] in the face of radical evil there is only dictatorship, and in such a moment the legitimist idea of hereditary succession becomes nothing but empty dogmatism."[33] "Radical evil" here is socialism, because "the revolutionary radicalism of the 1848 proletarian revolution" has been "infinitely more thorough and more consequential than the third estate's revolution of 1789."[34] And Cortés believes he needs to match this: "When the forces of attack are concentrating in political associations, then the forces of resistance necessarily also unite in one hand, without anybody being able to prevent it, or even allowed to prevent it. This is the clear, plausible, and incontestable theory of dictatorship."[35]

It rests on the promise that "the choice is not between freedom and dictatorship," but rather that it is about

---

29. Carl Schmitt, *Donoso Cortés in gesamteuropäischer Interpretation. Vier Aufsätze*. (Cologne: Greven, 1950), 21.

30. Juan Donoso Cortés, *Der Abfall vom Abendland* (Vienna: Herder, 1948), 32–33.

31. Ibid., 29.

32. Carl Schmitt, *Politische Theologie: Vier Kapitel zur Lehre von der Souveränität*, 2nd ed. (Munich: 1934), 83.

33. Ibid.

34. Ibid., 72.

35. Cortés, *Abfall vom Abendland*, 31.

choosing between a dictatorship of insurrection and a dictatorship of the Government. Faced with this question, I choose dictatorship of the Government because it is less oppressive and less disgraceful. One has to choose between either a dictatorship from above or a dictatorship from below. I choose the one from above, because it comes from a purer and more light-filled sphere. And finally, it is the choice between a dictatorship of the dagger and the dictatorship of the sword. I choose the dictatorship of the sword, because it is more honorable.[36]

In this way Cortés openly returns to something like the Roman barracks emperors in the form of a military dictatorship, but he still does so as an indeed *Constantinian* Catholic. He has an explicitly *Catholic* dictatorship in mind: the "shamelessly simple rule of the sword and the monk's cowl," to quote Karl Marx's *Eighteenth Brumaire of Louis Bonaparte*.[37] For Cortés the army and the church are the last two piers left standing in the revolutionary torrent. He frankly declares: "Today the standing armies are the only pillars that prevent civilization from falling back into barbarism."[38] And: the "most radical measure against revolution and socialism" is "Catholicism, and Catholicism alone." It is "the only doctrine that stands in absolute opposition to them."[39] Why? It is the religion that "instils charity in the rich and patience in the poor; that teaches the poor to content themselves and the rich to be merciful."[40] When looking at how he wants to solve the Social Question, one can see how Cortés has failed to understand it. The following words leave even less room for doubts about his sentiments: "The root of the evil is not the government, but the governed. For the evil is that the governed are less and less willing to let themselves be governed."[41]

Nonetheless, it would be a great mistake to simply cast Cortés aside (to the right) as an "extreme ... reactionary." More than that, as "the most radical counter-revolutionary"[42] of the nineteenth century, he was the first to discern in his theory of dictatorship an epochal reality, and of course this

36. Cortés cited in Robert Spaemann, *Der Ursprung der Soziologie aus dem Geist der Restauration: Studien über L.G.A. de Bonald* (Munich: Kösel, 1959), 171–72.

37. Karl Marx, *Der 18. Brumaire des Louis Bonaparte* (Frankfurt: Insel–Verlag, 1965), 13.

38. Cortés, *Abfall vom Abendland*, 78.

39. Ibid., 76.

40. Ibid., 63.

41. Ibid., 67.

42. Schmitt, *Donoso Cortés in gesamteuropäischer Interpretation*, 81.

was even easier since he himself desired it. However, as Schmitt emphasizes, the "authentic energy" of the concept of dictatorship lies in the "sphere of a revolutionary democratism" opposed to Cortés. It reduces any "system of conservative ideas and sentiments" to sheer absurdity, though it does so by logical necessity.[43]

The concept of dictatorship only truly comes full circle—as Schmitt is right to believe—in plebiscitary Caesarism, although this is not a democratic or even proletarian matter. It was in fact August Comte—the antisocialist and transformer of liberal theory into an authoritarian, that is "positivist" theory—who greeted Louis Napoleon's plebiscitary Caesarism as the solution to the 1848 revolutionary crisis. The abolition of the *régime parliamentaire* and the founding of the *république dictatorial* appeared to him like the *double préambule de toute vraie régénération*. For him Napoleon I was a tyrant for the sole reason that he had allied himself with a backward theology in support of his usurpation of power.[44]

Those coming after Napoleon will have no more need of this theology—not least because of Comte and his school. Or at least they will know how to clearly subdue it in such an alliance. Schmitt summarizes *ex eventu*: "Caesarism . . . is a typically non-Christian form of power even when it signs concordats."[45] What will remain—and significantly so—is the dictatorial state, although not a socialist one. Cortés has underestimated liberalism (i.e., he has taken its will to freedom too seriously). The Spanish Civil War, which he had predicted correctly—in addition to the dictatorship that arose with it—by no means crushed the (formerly) liberal citizens between its fronts. Almost all of them decided against socialism. Of course, at that moment, liberalism and its "chattering class" is dead (as a chattering class!). Cortés has painted its downfall in apocalyptic colors: "On that terror-filled day of struggle, when the decisive battle will be fought, when on the vast battlefield the immeasurable rows of Catholic troops and the hordes of socialists will be crashing back and forth, it will be asked in vain, and no one will be able to say what happened to liberalism."[46]

---

43. Carl Schmitt, "Donoso Cortes in Berlin (1849)," in *Wiederbegegnung von Kirche und Kultur in Deutschland: Eine Gabe für Karl Muth* (Munich: J. Kösel and F. Pustet, 1927), 338–73, 373.

44. Cf. Hans Barth, "Auguste Comte und Joseph des Maistre," *Schweizer Beiträge zur Allgemeinen Geschichte* 14 (1956), 103–38, 125–26.

45. Carl Schmitt, *Der Nomos der Erde im Völkerrecht des Jus Publicum Europaeum* (Berlin: Duncker and Humblot, 1950), 32.

46. Donoso Cortés, *Der Staat Gottes: Eine katholische Geschichtsphilosophie* [Ensayo

Political Demonology

Cortés is driven by the "martial idea of a bloody, definitive, annihilating, decisive battle."[47] As he is cornered by his position into the defense, it is the courage of despair (like dictatorship itself) that dictates his position to him. It is quite different with Proudhon, whom Cortés knows he stands eye-to-eye with, as enemies on a par with one another. But Proudhon, the representative of (anarcho-syndicalist) socialism (and one of George Sorel's most crucial teachers), is in the midst of a promising "destructive" attack: "In the eyes of Donoso . . . [Proudhon is] an evil demon, a devil."[48]

No doubt—and the sympathy of Carl Schmitt cited here only underlines this—with such an extreme juxtaposition Cortés has a "unique significance" for the future enemies of socialism: that of the anti-apocalypticist. Again in the words of Carl Schmitt, whom Taubes called the "apocalypticist of the *counter-revolution*":[49] "in the era of the relativizing dissolution of political concepts and oppositions, Donoso has" understood "the central concept of all great politics," and has held on to it "through all deceptive and fraudulent concealments," and has sought "to identify, beyond the distinctions of daily business of politics, the great historical and essential distinction between friend and enemy."[50]

It is a typical example of Schmitt's fake neutrality to simply talk about "friend and enemy." Otto Brunner pointed out a more than formal continuity when he registers Schmitt's "concept of the political," constructed from the friend-enemy opposition, "as merely . . . the endpoint in the development of a doctrine of *raison d'état*."[51] This last had always been *repressive*, both inwards and outwards. Once one knows the enemy Schmitt shares with Cortés, his formality unmistakably reveals what "devils" have to reckon with[52]: "The political enemy . . . is . . . the other, the alien, and it

---

sobre el Catolicismo, el Liberalismo y el Socialismo, Considerados en Sus Principios Fundamentals] translated and edited by Ludwig Fischer (Karlsruhe: Badenia, 1932), 200.

47. Schmitt, *Positionen und Begriffe*, 13.

48. Ibid., 14.

49. Jacob Taubes, "Carl Schmitt—ein Apokalyptiker der Gegenrevolution," in *Die Tgeszeitung*, 20.07.1985, 10–11.

50. Schmitt, *Donoso Cortés in gesamteuropäischer Interpretation*, 78.

51. Cited after Schmitt, *The Concept of the Political*, 14.

52. *The Concept of the Political* was written on the eve of German fascism, out of and into a situation of civil war. A 1939 essay referring back to the extended 1932 version of *The Concept of the Political* explicitly identifies "depoliticization," which Cortés already opposed, with "indecision, nihilism and in the end bolshevism" ("Neutralität und Neutralisierung. Zu Christoph Steding Das Reich und die Krankheit der europäischen

suffices for his essence that he is essentially something different and alien in a particularly intensive sense, so that in the extreme case conflicts with him are possible, which can neither be decided by a general advance standardization, nor by the judgment of a third party that is 'uninvolved' and hence 'impartial.'"[53]

Even earlier, de Bonald, the key teacher of Cortés and also Schmitt, noted: *"Je me trouve constamment entre deux abimes, je marche toujours entre l'être et le néant."*[54] So for him the "extreme case" had already become a permanent situation, that is, decisionism had become permanent: "Wherever Catholic philosophy of the 19th century appears in contemporary intellectual form, it expresses in one way or another the thought that a great alternative arises, allowing for no mediation. No medium, says [Cardinal] Newman, between catholicity and atheism. All of them define a great Either-Or, the rigour of which ... rings of dictatorship."[55]

Schmitt, who has been paraphrased and cited here throughout, completes this thought and does away with it.[56] As we have heard, in 1949–50 he wanted more than ever to help ensure "that now, for the third time, Donoso's name is no more left unheard, and that his speech unfolds its power."

With words to a similar effect, the Regensburg Bishop Michael Buchberger, editor of the first *Lexikon für Theologie und Kirche*, had already in 1932–33 greeted the German translation of Cortés's *Essay on Catholicism, Liberalism, and Socialism*: "With the sharp visionary eye of the deeply faithful scholar, Donoso Cortés was one of the first to understand the meaning and admonition lying in the socialist movement and the social revolution.

Kultur." *Deutsche Rechtswissenschaft* IV (1939), volume 2, 97).

53. Schmitt, *Der Begriff des Politischen*, 27.

54. "I constantly find myself between two abysses; I always tread between being and nothingness." Cited in Schmitt, *Politische Theologie: Vier Kapitel zur Lehre von der Souveränität* (Munich: Duncker and Humblot, 1922), 50; cf. also Joseph de Maistre, *Vom Papste*, 2 vols. (Munich: Allgemeine Verlagsanstalt München, 1923), 195.

55. Schmitt, *Politische Theologie* (1934), 69.

56. *Translators' note: Faber uses the word *aufheben*, which retains the double-sided Hegelian connotation of 'abolition' and 'preservation.' Already in 1948 Alfred von Martin, who has unjustifiably been forgotten, called Schmitt "the last of the political theologians"; cf. Martin, *Im Zeichen der Humanität: Soziologische Streifzüge* (Frankfurt: Knecht, 1974), 130; and more recently: Richard Faber and Perdita Ladwig (eds.), *Gesellschaft und Humanität: der Kultursoziologe Alfred von Martin (1882–1979)* (Würzburg: Königshausen & Neumann, 2013).

Because of this, his work remains timely and valuable even today and especially today."[57]

When it comes to the period after 1945, one can hardly over-emphasize that the Schmitt essay cited above was first printed in 1949 in the journal *Die neue Ordnung* [The New Order], edited at the then-influential Dominican monastery in Walberberg. In that same year, there also appeared a contribution by Schmitt's Catholic student Günther Krauss, "The Totalitarian Idea of the State," which openly spells out why Cortés is still, or rather more than ever, "timely": "Donoso Cortés already predicted our situation a hundred years ago: the dictatorship of the proletariat as the connection between socialism and Slavdom. What was his antidote to this dictatorship? Dictatorship." And Krauss poses the further rhetorical question: "Do we even have a choice between totalitarianism and non-totalitarianism?" His apodictic answer is: "on the field of worldviews he who fights at half speed and with empty hands has no chance, and on top of that he is busy with other things, such as denazification. What counts here is faith against faith, spearhead against spearhead, as it says in the Song of Hildebrand, myth against myth, as one [still today] has to say"[58] (in agreement with Alfred Rosenberg, down to the spelling of *Mythus*).

2. THE ROMAN CATHOLIC AND ROMAN-ATHEIST COUNTER-REVOLUTION, ESPECIALLY CHARLES MAURAS'S

Krauss' continuity with the "epoch of fascism" (Ernst Nolte) is more than evident; it is explicit, although (in our present context) I am not very keen on the concept of fascism. The self-definition as "conservative revolutionaries" common amongst all (pre- and pro-)fascists suffices, certainly enough to quote and agree with Jean F. Neurohr:

> Since 1789, since de Maistre [and de Bonald], since the Legitimists and the Romantic Conservatives, . . . there had always been something Satanic, something Luciferian about the word "revolution"; it had meant a rebellion against the eternal order of God. However, after 1918 there was heroic ring to the word, it became something great, something permitted, indeed . . . necessary, ordained by

---

57. Cf. J. Donoso Cortés, *Der Staat Gottes*, Preface.

58. Günther Krauss, "Die totalitäre Staatsidee," *Die neue Ordnung* (1949), 494–508, 497–98.

God, when the aim was ... to establish through revolution ... the conditions under which life could be dignified and worth living again.[59]

It is precisely the "*Conservative* Revolution" which, "according to a felicitous... definition by Edgar Jung, smashes temporal institutions into pieces in order to preserve *eternal orders*."[60]

This last quoted Leopold Ziegler, a popular philosopher quite influential via his sometime favorite student Edgar Julius Jung (private secretary to Franz von Papen), who did Catholicize to an extent, but (like Jung) he remained a (wayward) Protestant throughout his life. It should be pointed out emphatically that Neurohr spoke not only with a view to Catholic Conservative Revolutionaries, despite mentioning de Maistre and the "Romantic Conservatives" by name. Indeed, these last were not, in general, Catholics by denomination. And a lot of the "modern" or indeed "revolutionary" Conservatives have completely ceased to be Christians; they may well even be *Antichristians*. And the fact that they are so partly in a Catholicizing sense is not a contradiction at all, as nobody proves more compellingly than Charles Maurras, who also heavily influenced Carl Schmitt.[61]

Indeed Maurras' doctrine is a "doctrine of the fear-instilling, hateful enemy"[62]—including the special characteristic in common with Schmitt's friend/enemy theory, which is to trace this enemy down to his earliest forms of historical appearance. Maurras talks extensively about the "difficulty" posed by "neutralising the infinite and absolute principle... Perhaps the solution is to establish worldly authorities aimed at channelling and tempering this horrible meddling of the divine. This is what Catholicism does."[63]

This is what it has always done; it is its essence, and the French essence was also of this kind—up until the Revolution; up until the Reformation it was the occidental essence. The (bourgeois) Revolution, and today socialism ,are the ever radicalising waves of the flood of Judeo-Christian anarchism

---

59. Jean Frederic Neurohr, *Der Mythos vom Dritten Reich: zur Geistesgeschichte des Nationalsozialismus* (Stuttgart: Cotta, 1957), 74.

60. Leopold Ziegler, "Der deutsche Staat," *Deutsche Rundschau* 238–39 (1934), 133–43, 137.

61. Cf. Helmut Quaritsch, *Positionen und Begriffe Carl Schmitts*, 2nd ed. (Berlin: Duncker and Humblot, 1991), 64.

62. Ernst Nolte, *Der Faschismus in seiner Epoche: die Action française, der italienische Faschismus, der Nationalsozialismus*, 2nd ed. (Munich: Piper, 1965), 186.

63. Cited in ibid.

which in the end, after 1200 years, destroys the Catholic "channelling" of the divine: what was once the "Christian-Catholic substance of Europe" has broken apart into its constituent pieces, and the "Catholic" part, in which the once-integral paganism continues to exist, has been pushed into the defensive corner. Though just in this way it is the only force that a new—political—paganism can rely on: *"Je suis athée, mais je suis catholique."*

Maurras confesses atheism, disregarding tactical considerations in favor of strategy i.e., logical necessity. In *Chemin de Paradis* he poses the rhetorical question "whether the idea of God, the only one and the one present to consciousness, is always a beneficent and political idea ... if one allows this naturally anarchic consciousness to develop the sense that it could make a direct connection with the absolute and infinite being, then the idea of this invisible and remote Lord will quickly obliterate the respect it owes to its visible and close lord: rather than men, it will prefer to obey God."[64]

This Apostolic maxim (Acts 5:29) which Maurras directly attacks here is the inheritance of Jewish prophetism, as is early Christianity as a whole. Prophetism, the "inventor" of monotheism, remains the root of all evils. At first it is active in the Reformation's reception of Christianity, since for Maurras Protestantism is nothing but the re-awakening of an original and anarchical Christianity, "which only in the imposed form of Roman-imperatorial paganism could become the protagonist of authority."[65]

Maurras' argument may be summarized in the words of Ernst Nolte as follows:

> If the Reformation means nothing but "the unleashed tumult of the inner life," if it is nothing but an anarchist attack on the civilization of Rome, then it has to have its roots outside Rome, in a barbaric-anarchist, anti-Roman phenomenon. As Maurras adopts Protestantism's self-understanding, putting a contrary accent on it, he finds this phenomenon in early Christianity. It is nothing but a form of Jewish prophetism, whose anti-civilizational and primitivist character [Ernest] Renan had described. Hostility to civilization connects the "Hebrew desert" with the "Germanic primeval forest": the cry of the prophet awakens in the German the unfettered rage of his instincts, biblicism and Germanism become one in the barbarity of modernity. And with this, the well-known thesis that freedom and democracy had their origins

---

64. Cited in ibid.
65. Ibid., 69.

in Old Germania gains a new and strange emphasis. Democracy, which had developed in the forests of Germania, was right to accept nourishment and approval from that Christianity of Jesus the Jew, who [again according to Renan, but also Nietzsche] had been an anarchic enthusiast: "The fathers of the Revolution are in Geneva, in Wittenberg, and at earlier times in Jerusalem; they are drawing on the Jewish spirit and the varieties of an independent Christianity, which were raging in the oriental deserts and the primeval forests of Germania, at different focal points of barbarity." Yet this Judaism is not only a distant historical root; it may be found freshly alive and unchanged in the modern world: "The Jew, monotheist and nourished by the prophets, has become an agent of the Revolution." Rome had found ways to neutralise the "poison of the Magnificat," as medieval society had known how to confine and to make use of the Jews, but Protestantism and the Revolution have torn down the barriers, and the rebellious barbarian threateningly stands within the walls of a society deeply shaken.[66]

For Maurras the idea of progress, the historical-philosophical motif of all enlightenment, of all idealism, positivism, and socialism, means "a barely secularized messianism." Mediated by Protestantism, Enlightenment philosophy was altogether a fruit from the Jewish tree. German Idealism was also nothing but the most sublime formation of Jewish-Christian monotheism, analogous to science [*Wissenschaft*], at least where it did not submit itself to serve higher interests. Its system consisted in replacing the God of the Jews with curiosity, which was unfittingly called "Science," which sat on an altar as the centre of the world, and which was paid the same honors as Yahweh.

Yet the development inaugurated by this modern spirit is coming to a bad end only today in socialism, the most radical form of "slave rebellion," as Maurras—conforming with Nietzsche—reinterprets the emancipatory history of modern times. And because socialism was the eschatological intensification of a principle that had been in power in France since 1789, it was insufficient to fight it alone; one could destroy socialism only if one destroyed its allied predecessors together with it, the complete "Left." According to Maurras the Left is not only a group of revolutionaries and the masses that follow them. Even the future *Volksfront* far from covers this

---

66. Ibid., 170.

"Left" he has in mind. All republicans, all liberals are "Reds," pioneers of the "egalitarian barbarity" against whom a barricade must be erected.[67]

As if there could be no question about it, Maurras thinks the army are those who have to stand on this side of the barricade: "In France one can posit the axiom 'No army, no public order.' The Mr. Radicals, Mr. Socialists, and Mr. Communists would then be the masters of all." Yet this consequence must be thwarted. To an extent Maurras propagates and organizes the civil war from the right. "However deep his aversion even against terrorism may be, still he is not afraid . . . to talk . . . about conservative revolution. Radical reaction is a revolution against the revolution." Emphatically, in Maurras' own words: "*Au nom de la raison et de la nature, conformément aux vieilles lois de l'univers, pour le salut de l'ordre, pour la durée et les progres d'une civilisation menace, toutes les espérances flottent sur le navire d'une Contre-Revolution.*"[68]

The "names" in which the (counter-)revolution is to be waged once again signal the fundamentals of Maurras' fight: "cis-cendence" against transcendence, and, with a view to history, archaism. Maurras wants to apprehend where "counter-nature" had its beginnings, in Judeo-Christianity, and he wants to do so with the help of the institution that domesticated it first (albeit not for good): the Catholic Church and its societal system. Its "shells" would be its "armor" against the assaults of modernity, led by Judeo-Christianity.[69]

Only as a pagan Catholic, critically formed by the Laicist Catholicism of Comte (i.e., only as a biologist), can Maurras preserve ancient, Catholic heritage: the latter as the former, and the former only in so far as it serves him as evidence of the "beautiful inequalities," which "make what is beautiful beautiful, the state strong, and the people healthy." For Maurras human nature only exists in a synchronic plural, as differences: higher and lower natures.[70]

According to its very concept, order is command and submission: "hierarchy." It would be easier to grasp, easier to defend, if every being,

---

67. Cf. ibid., 158.

68. Cf. ibid., 157 and 179, as well as Ernst Robert Curtius, *Der Syndicalismus der Geistesarbeiter in Frankreich* (Bonn: F. Cohen, 1921), 16. *Translators' note: *In the name of reason and nature, conforming to the ancient laws of the universe, all hopes are floating on the ship of a Counter-Revolution.*

69. Cf. Armin Mohler, *Die französische Rechte: vom Kampf um Frankreichs Ideologienpanzer* (Munich: Isar Verlag, 1958), 42.

70. Cf. Nolte, *Der Faschismus in seiner Epoche*, 183–84.

according to its greater or lesser capabilities, were to serve order from its place and there were to find its own proper fulfillment. This is roughly the idea of the orthodox-Catholic doctrine of order. However, it presupposes a different, more idealistic idea of the world than does Maurras, a reader of Lucretius. For *him*, it is not a logical consequence of each one's nature that some human atoms are forever locked into interior darkness, whilst others are "happily" enjoying the light. Rather, the fate of each atom is mere chance, and it is only from this chance that the unique lucky strike of beauty and perfection arises—which for Lucretius is the world, but for Maurras the well-ordered society: the whole world, he writes, would be less good "if it had contained fewer mysterious sacrifices made for the sake of its perfection." Maurras identifies the atoms locked into the dark as human sacrifices necessary for the perfection of society. But like Lucretius he presupposes that the respective position on the social ladder has aleatory grounds. Only this mechanistic presupposition then gives the Maurrasian doctrine of order its unique—if you will, positivist—accent. And "positivist" in the case of Maurras, going beyond Comte, has to be understood as "related to blood." His mechanics are a bio-logic: it is blood, the "substance of substances," that allocates the various positions and so guarantees to each family—befitting their social rank—the continuity of their position: "As long as men are created through blood and the blood is shed in battle, the actual political order will be administered through blood."[71]

Beyond Comte, Maurras is a neo-feudalist and, on the grounds of his naturalism, a racist. Only when neo-paganism is "perfected" in social-biologism does fascism *sans phrase* appear: some form of an "SS-state." Its anti-intellectuals, such as (indirectly) the later Maurras, who rose to become chief ideologue of Vichy France, represent the extreme counter-position to human(itarian)ists of all stripes. One may regard Thomas Mann's Naphta as his ideal prologue in every respect, the great nemesis of "civilization's man of letters" Settembrini, and even more than that, Naphta's crucial prototype Ludwig Derleth.[72] I shall remind the reader here that Schmitt's Jesuit friend Erich Przywara (in 1936) interpreted Derleth as the "black-Nietzschean"

---

71. Cf. ibid., 161 and 184.

72. Cf. Gerhard Loose, "Naphta: Über das Verhältnis von Prototyp und dichterischer Gestalt in Thomas Manns 'Zauberberg,'" in *Ideologiekritische Studien zur Literatur. Essays I*, edited by Volkmar Sander (Frankfurt: Athenäum, 1972), 215–50, as well as Richard Faber, "Die politisch–religiösen Ideendichter Ludwig Derleth, Stefan George, und Henrik Ibsen," in *Ibsens "Kaiser und Galiläer": Quellen, Interpretationen, Rezeptionen*, edited by Faber and Helge Høibraaten (Würzburg: Königshausen & Neumann, 2011), 181–209.

endpoint of a line beginning with Donoso Cortés—like Derleth, a Jesuit *manqué*—but going back even further.⁷³ Still in 1956 Przywara calls this line "Ignatian,"⁷⁴ not least because of its *dualistic* theology of history. In just the same way Thomas Mann's Naphta (adapted from Derleth) "carries" it "before himself" when he speaks "of the '*dos banderas*,'" of "the 'two flags,' around which the armies gather for the great campaign: the hellish and the spiritual one; one in the region of Jerusalem, where Christ, the '*capitan general*' of the good, is commander—the other in the plains of Babylon, where Lucifer poses as '*caudillo*' or chieftain."⁷⁵

Whoever has seen "the two flags flying," whoever "has seen Christ in the field and Satan on his throne," for him—so the Ignatian inference by Przywara's friend Reinhold Schneider—"no choice remains; there is only one command that he can follow. The power and the will of the servant become one. The will of the leader [*Führer*] is pointing in one direction."⁷⁶— "As the first king-leader of the military ever ... [Christ Imperator Maximus] has ordered man to lead a heroic life," as Derleth(-Naphta) will still declare in "The Death of Thanatos" in 1945.⁷⁷ In terms of (religious) politics this was done in the service of the counter-Reformation (and counter-revolutionary) Rome; already the Jesuit order "as the irreconcilable enemy of the new"⁷⁸ had fought under its signs, and indeed it had done so "in a draconian, almost military centralization of values."⁷⁹ Schneider summarizes: "To the (Protestant-)Nordic rejoicing over the fall of the barriers, the (Catholic) south responds with a hammer-blow onto the foundation stone of an even stricter building."⁸⁰

---

73. Erich Przywara, *Heroisch* (Paderborn: Schöningh, 1936).

74. Erich Przywara, *Ignatianisch: Vier Studien zum 400. Todestag des Heiligen Ignatius von Loyola* (Frankfurt: Knecht, 1956).

75. Thomas Mann, *Der Zauberberg: Roman*. 7th ed. (Berlin: Fischer, 1964), 409, as well as Faber, "Preußischer Katholizismus und katholisches Preußentum," in *Preußische Katholiken und katholische Preußen im 20. Jahrhundert*, edited by Faber and Uwe Puschner (Würzburg: Königshausen & Neumann, 2011), 89–114.

76. Reinhold Schneider, *Philipp der Zweite, oder Religion und Macht* (Frankfurt: Suhrkamp, 1987), 88.

77. Ludwig Derleth, *Der Tod des Thanatos* (Luzern: Stocker, 1945), C. 48.

78. Schneider, *Philipp der Zweite*, 89.

79. Hermann Broch, *Der Zerfall der Werte*, in: *Gesammelte Werke*, vol. 7 (Zürich: Rhein-Verlag 1955), 29.

80. Schneider, *Philipp der Zweite*, 116.

3. EUHEMERISTIC THEISM, OR RATHER: CATHOLIC ATHEISM

Maurras was also a resolute anti-Protestant, yet—as we have also already heard—in such a radical manner that his anti-Reformation disposition included an anti-Christian and anti-Jewish, that is an *anti*-monotheistic disposition. So at least in this regard, does Maurras not stand in contradiction to his (perhaps only partial) student Schmitt? He was also an uncompromising anti-Protestant (despite, or because of his Hobbesianism),[81] but what about Schmitt's monotheism, which is central for us? Did he not simply, even emphatically, fight against what is effectively a doctrine of *two* gods? Yes, but with the obvious premise that not even the doctrine of the Trinity, regarded as a panacea by his opponent Erik Peterson, necessarily prevented an inner-divine "stasis."[82] For Schmitt, the turn from Political (Mono-)Theology into Political(-dualist) Christology (i.e., "stasiology") is possible *at all times*: "The structural core problem of the Gnostic dualism between a god of creation and a god of redemption governs . . . every religion of salvation and redemption" from the very beginning and *permanently so*: because it "structurally" inheres in it (not to mention that "in every world in need of change and renewal" this problem "is immanently given"). But then, does one not *have to* become an atheist like Maurras (or at least a polytheist in the way of Max Weber, Hans Blumenberg, and Odo Marquard[83])?

---

81. Cf. Siegfried Lokatis, "Wilhelm Stapel und Carl Schmitt–Ein Briefwechsel." In *Schmittiana: Beiträge zu Leben und Werk Carl Schmitts*, vol. 5, edited by Piet Tommissen (Berlin: Duncker and Humblot, 1996).

82. Cf. Schmitt, *Politische Theologie II*, 63.

83. Cf. Max Weber, *Wissenschaft als Beruf*, Berlin 1967 (critical towards Weber: Jacob Taubes, "Kultur und Ideologie" [1969], in *Vom Kult zur Kultur: Bausteine zu einer Kritik der historischen Vernunft* [Munich: Fink, 1996] 283ff., and Richard Faber, "Politische Psychologie: Ovids 'Metamorphosen' in aktuellem Kontext," in *Foedera Naturai. Klaus Heinrich zum 60. Geburtstag*, edited by Hartmut Zinser et al. [Würzburg: Königshausen & Neumann, 1989] 103–18); Hans Blumenberg, *Arbeit am Mythos* (Frankfurt: Suhrkamp, 1979); Odo Marquard, "Lob des Polytheismus," in Marquard, *Abschied vom Prinzipiellen* (Stuttgart: Reclam, 1981), 91ff, and Marquard, "Aufgeklärter Polytheismus– auch eine politische Theologie." In *Der Fürst dieser Welt: Carl Schmitt und die Folgen*, edited by Jacob Taubes, 2nd ed. (Munich: Fink, 1985), 77ff. Critical towards Blumenberg and Marquard: Richard Faber, *Der Prometheus-Komplex: Zur Kritik der Politotheologie Eric Voegelins und Hans Blumenbergs* (Würzburg: Königshausen & Neumann, 1984); Teil (below as Excursus I); as well as Jacob Taubes, "Zur Konjunktur des Polytheismus," (1983) in Taubes, *Vom Kult zur Kultur*, 340ff.

I cannot see that Schmitt theoretically (or explicitly) ever took this step. Instead he more or less always confessed to be a "Eusebius *redivivus*":[84] an almost "monarchic" Catholic, completely assimilating Christ to the Father, decisively Roman in almost having the latter absorb the former, indeed Constantinian, that is, a *caesaro-papist* Catholic. The epitome of such a Catholicism, and equally every hierocratic and hence total(itarian) Catholicism, is the *Christus Imperator, Rex et Victor*, whom Schmitt explicitly invokes (just as the Roman imperial coronation liturgy of the Middle Ages did). Here I will cite, of course, Reinhold Schneider's 1931 characterization of the "Christ-*Führer*"; Schneider, who had then not yet reverted to faith, accomplished it with a view to the *Byzantine* Christ Pantocrator of Cefalu: "Ruler and judge, no longer with the serenity of suffering, but with the serenity of *power*. He is at once Creator and Redeemer, Father and Son—Redeemer perhaps only because He created. In the movement of his hand, in his gaze, there is a merciless demand that love cannot fulfill, that is perhaps even indifferent to it. He came in order to coerce allegiance. By opening the Scriptures and pointing, his robe only slightly unfolded: merely by revealing himself he brings about the *decision* no one can escape."[85]

Schneider sees the very Christ that for Schmitt is also represented by the Roman Catholic Church, its papacy above all: the "reigning, ruling, triumphant Christ."[86] He is that Christ-Father who for Schmitt does *not* arise against the God-Father and so—inner-divinely—will not start the revolution.[87] It is the God of Pope Gregory the Great, whom Schmitt then cites approvingly: "God is highest power and highest being. All power is from him, and is, and remains divine and good in its essence. Should the devil have power, this power is, as far as it is above all divine power, divine and good. Only the will of the devil is evil. Yet despite this eternal evil, satanic will, the power itself remains divine and good."[88]

The Christ Pantocrator of Cefalu, for example, is and remains above all the "Byzantine" one, before the occidental "Fall," the "schism of the world . . . into the historical dualism of holy and profane, of church and

---

84. Cf. Schmitt, *Politische Theologie II*, 28.

85. Reinhold Schneider, *Schicksal und Landschaft* (Freiburg/Br.: Herder, 1960), 178.

86. Schmitt, *Römischer Katholizismus und Politische Form*, 2nd ed. (Munich: Theatiner Verlag, 1925), 65–66.

87. Cf. Schmitt, *Politische Theologie II*, 120–21.

88. Cited after Carl Schmitt, *Gespräch über die Macht und den Zugang zum Machthaber* (Pfullingen: Neske 1954), 21.

empire, of priesthood and aristocracy"; this schism already carries within itself "the seed of the future desanctification of state and politics"[89] and so founds the *general* disappearance of authority. Derleth radically faces it, i.e., he strives for an *integral* resacralization (by way of the papal church), and in his "Christus Imperator Maximus" (dated 1905 and 1919) he invokes precisely the "Christ of Cefalu." His soldiers declare: "We unconditionally surrender to the *leader* [*Führer*] with the baton of command, who with inextinguishable fires destroys once and for all the groundwork of the makeshift in-between kingdom, because he walks in advance of the heir of the *Fisherman's Ring*, who builds his church upon this rock and is expected as the king and the redeemer of the world and the savior of time."[90]

Christ is "leader," "commander," "pope," "king and world redeemer": all the monarchist titles relevant in the past, present, and future are heaped upon this one who—particularly as the *"complexio oppositorum"*—anticipates that "Führer," "the cry" for whom "is trembling through people conscious of their nation," as Eugen Rosenstock-Huessy writes in his and Josef Wittig's "The Age of the *Church*" in 1928.[91] Schmitt would have been the last to ignore the caesarist mood at the time; he promoted it by "rationalizing" it and saw his prophecy of the *"new"* order" fulfilled in the "New *Kingdom* [*Reich*]" of the "Augustus" Hitler, the kingdom—in the Maistrian/Schmittian sense—of the political "pope," as the "charismatic leader"—in the Weberian sense.

We will leave aside here Schmitt's fascism, or rather national socialism, and concentrate on the fact that Derleth, highly respected by theologians such as Przywara and Hans Urs von Balthasar, was a *hierocrat* and hence played a role which could be taken up by Schmitt at times, and indeed *was* taken up by him. "To set the evocation of a religious-moral world dictatorship of the church against the utopia of a communist-socialist future state,"[92] as the German integralist Otfried Eberz had desired in 1922, "was more than *aesthetically* attractive"—to go back to the editorial note by *Hochland*'s editor Karl Muth on Eberz's essay "Catholic Imperialism." But because Schmitt's friend Eberz hierocratically emphasized the medieval

---

89. Karl Anton Prinz Rohan, "Adel im Wandel der Zeiten," *Die Besinnung* 12 (1957), 166–69, 167.

90. Ludwig Derleth, *Proklamationen*, 2nd ed. (Munich: Musarion, 1919), 89.

91. Eugen Rosenstock-Huessy and Josef Wittig, *Das Alter der Kirche* (Berlin–Dahlem: Verlag L. Schneider, 1927), 5 [emphasis added].

92. Otfried Eberz, "Katholischer Imperialismus," *Hochland* XX (1922), 55.

"*world*-idea of the Christian empire," his anti-utopia was also a bad utopia (i.e., a sheer impossibility). By the same token it was once again openly articulated what the "systemic" *telos* of Catholicism actually was *and* is: the Catholic Church is "a theocracy . . . and its politics" towards "states" was "never anything else but theocratic imperialism."[93]

"The Church"—to let Schmitt himself speak here—"like every other imperialism spanning the world, will, when it has reached its aim, bring peace to the world, but a fear hostile to all form discerns in this peace the victory of the devil."[94] And not only did men of letters such as Schmitt and Eberz "medievally" regard the opposite to be correct: "with Pius XI's first encyclical '*Ubi arcano*' and its pontifical theme, the *Pax Christi in Regno Christi*, dated 23 December 1922,"[95] "the political form" of Roman Catholicism had also officially "reached a peak," as Hans Barion, the canonist of the Schmitt School, writes in 1968. Besides the Lateran Accords of 1929 Barion calls the peak's "most significant manifestation" the 1925 introduction of the Feast of *Christ* the King.[96]

This introduction is not merely to be judged from an intra-ecclesial point of view, if that is ever even possible, but for the time being it marks—to papalistically emphasize this—the intra-ecclesial final peak of the pope's "*Christificatio*" as the "*vicarius Christi*."[97] No doubt it is under the influence of Pius XI's pontificate that the English convert Theophilus Stephan Gregory writes in 1938: "The *Vicarius Christi* is the most powerful symbol of man's submission to Christ."[98] This is exactly what Boniface VIII means when—in Schneider's "Great Renunciation"—he calls out with fanatical incitement: "This is Anagni, the City in which the Vicar of Christ was slapped in the face—and so was Christ through him."[99] Eberz affirms in 1922: Philip

---

93. Ibid.

94. Schmitt, *Römischer Katholizismus und politische Form*, 66.

95. Hans Barion, "'Weltgeschichtliche Machtform'?," in *Epirrhosis: Festgabe für Carl Schmitt*, edited by Hans Barion et al. (Berlin: Duncker and Humblot, 1968), 19.

96. Ibid.

97. Cf. Fritz Leist, *Der Gefangene des Vatikans: Strukturen der päpstlichen Herrschaft* (Munich: Kösel, 1971), 95.

98. Theophilus Stephan Gregory, *Das unvollendete Universum: Schicksalsgestaltung der abendländischen Geschichte*, trans. and introd. by Oskar Bauhofer (Einsiedeln: Benziger, 1938), 275. [*The Unfinished Universe*; retranslated from the German]

99. Reinhold Schneider, "Der große Verzicht," in *Homo Viator: Modernes christliches Theater* (Cologne: J. Hegner, 1962), 368.

the Fair "smashed to pieces . . . in Anagni the theocratic world empire of the lawgiver of Nazareth."[100]

We will dwell on Eberz's words on the ecclesial "theocracy," which in 1926 for example were shared by Nuntius Eugenio Pacelli (later Pius XII) when he calls the church of Christ a "supernatural and spiritual theocracy."[101] Schmitt, unlike almost everyone else, insisted on its *juridical* character; again in *Roman Catholicism and Political Form* he says: "The pope is not the prophet, but the *vicar* of Christ. All fanatic wildness of unfettered prophecy is kept at bay through such a formulation. In this way, as the office is made *independent* from charisma, the priest gains a dignity that seems to fully abstract from a concrete person." This latter point may be true, yet nonetheless the office itself is a charisma. It is given with the office, but without the reversal of this relationship having become impossible. As Schmitt himself has to write, priesthood and papacy both go back "in an unbroken chain to the *personal* mission and the *person* of Christ,"[102] no doubt an extremely charismatic one. The charismatic component cannot be fully excluded from any Christianity, which includes the Catholic one, even though its tendency certainly is anticharismatic and juridical, defusing charisma not by merely negating it, but by binding it to an administration [*Be-amtentum*].

Schmitt had already written in 1914's *The Value of the State* that "the infallible pope, the . . . most Absolute that may be conceived on earth, is nothing by virtue of his person, but is only a vicar of *Christ* on earth."[103] As regards the pure instrumentality of the papal office holder (which that section also mentions), who took up the old title of "*servus servorum Dei*," one should recall what Hugo Ball wrote in a 1924 review, endorsed by Schmitt as late as 1970: Schmitt's "tendency towards the Absolute in its final consequence does not lead to an originary abstraction, be it called God, form, authority, or whatever, but rather to the *pope* as the absolute person."[104]

De Maistre before him had hypothetically relied on the fact that papalism is nothing but politics, which shows precisely how Schmitt is "the

---

100. Eberz, "Katholischer Imperialismus," 59.

101. Cited after Pius XII, *Der Papst an die Deutschen: Pius XII, als Apostolischer Nuntius und als Papst in seinen deutsch—sprachigen Reden und Sendschreiben von 1917–1956*, edited by Bruno Wuestenberg (Frankfurt: Scheffler, 1956), 43.

102. Schmitt, *Römischer Katholizismus und Politische Form*, 29–30.

103. Schmitt, *Der Wert des Staates und die Bedeutung des Einzelnen*, Tübingen 1914, 95.

104. Hugo Ball, "Carl Schmitt's Politische Theologie," *Hochland* XXI (1924), 264.

last of the political theologians,"[105] especially in view of de Maistre, de Bonald, and Donoso Cortés. In a letter to the Archbishop of Ragusa, de Maistre wrote: "*Si j'étais athée et souverain, . . . je déclarerais le pape infaillible par edit public, pour l'établissement et la sûreté dans mes états. En effet, il peut y avoir quelques raisons de se battre, de s'égorger même pour les fables, il n'y aurait pas de plus grande duperie.*"[106]

It may be a mere fiction, but it is revealing. Hans Barth is right to comment on this passage as follows: "The absolutization of the idea of social order and the idea of unity of religious doctrine, which is at the basis of order, gives rise to the danger that the inner justification of the doctrine within the idea of truth is given hardly any attention and is no more felt to be an immediate need."[107]

As Schmitt formulated juridically in his 1922 *Political Theology*: the authority "to make law does not have to be in the right."[108] And no doubt papal infallibility is in particular also a question of (ecclesiastical) law. De Maistre circles around the idea that unity prevails only where there is a single organ that somehow continuously creates and preserves, administers, and interprets it. This *authority* in the figure of the pope is *"le chef naturel, le promoteur le plus puissant, le grand Démiurg de la civilisation universelle."*[109]

To cite de Maistre's general thesis here: *"Il ne peut y avoir de societé humaine sans gouvernement, ni de gouvernement sans souverainté, ni de souverainté sans infaillibilité; et ce dernier privilège est meme dans les souveraintés temporelles (où n'est pas) sous peine de voir l'association se dissoudre."*[110] "[So] 'the worldly as well as the spiritual order' needs a 'power that judges but is itself not judged,' a power that decides all possible conflicts, be they

---

105. Cf. von Martin, *Im Zeichen der Humanität*.

106. "If I were atheist and sovereign, . . . I would declare the Pope infallible by public edict, for the establishment and the safety in my states. Indeed, there may be some reasons to struggle, to slaughter each other even for the fables, there would be no greater deceit." Cited in Barth, "Auguste Comte und Joseph des Maistre," 119.

107. Ibid.

108. Schmitt, *Politische Theologie* (1934), 20.

109. ". . . the natural chief, the most powerful promoter, the great Demiurge of the universal civilization." Cited after H. Barth, "Auguste Comte und Joseph des Maistre," 121.

110. "There can be no human society without government, no government without sovereignty, no sovereignty without infallibility; and this last privilege exists even in the temporal sovereignties (where it is not) under pain of seeing the association dissolve." Cited after ibid.

of a spiritual or political origin and kind, and does so in the last instance, 'sans appel,' and hence finally and bindingly."[111]

Barth's comment here again puts the finger on the essential decisionism of de Maistre's papalism, and not only de Maistre's. In effect, the papalist analogy only serves to manipulate "infallibility" as "the essence of the unappealable decision." That the two words "infallibility" and "sovereignty" are *"parfaitement synonymes"* (*Du Pape*, ch. 1) means: "In practice" there is no difference "between not being in error . . . [and] being exempt from being tried for error; what matters is that no higher authority can repeal the decision"[112]—as it says in, again, Schmitt's *Political Theology* (I).

But in a (Catholic) church-specific sense, does this not mean that, to use Maurras' words one last time, "Catholicism eliminates the Father as much as the Son" and declares *itself* to be the "guardian of man?"[113] Schmitt personally was repeatedly compared to Dostoyevski's "Grand Inquisitor,"[114] and for his part he defended him.[115] Yet we are never merely concerned with the *ecclesial*-Catholic, but rather, for example in the following section with the monarchist emphasis on unity in general (not only Schmitt's), even if no less an authority than Jacob Burckhard has attributed[116] it to the Catholic Church above all other institutions. On the other hand, even the Catholic Church, or indeed precisely the Catholic Church, has never been safe from schism and heresy. And with the emperor, or rather the state, the papacy engages in a (slightly war-like) *perpetual* fight. In other words: caesaro-papism and hierocracy are *bad* utopias, because (in the long run) they are *sheer* impossibilities.

4. CHURCH-STATE DUALISM

Sub specie "Political Christology," or rather *demonology*, it also means that there is a pope-emperor dualism, or rather: church-state dualism—always

---

111. Ibid., 120–21.

112. Schmitt, *Politische Theologie* (1934), 71–72.

113. Cf. Nolte, *Der Faschismus in seiner Epoche*, 187.

114. Cf. Alfred Schindler and Frithard Scholz, "Die Theologie Carl Schmitts," in *Der Fürst dieser Welt*, edited by Jacob Taubes (Munich: Fink), 153–73, 172–73.

115. Schmitt, *Politische Theologie* (1934), 74, and *Römischer Katholizismus* (Hellerau: Hegner, 1923), 66–67.

116. Cf. Jacob Burckhardt, *Weltgeschichtliche Betrachtungen*, (Munich: n.d.), 179.

theologically articulated, if not generated. In the words of Schmitt from his *Political Theology II*:

> The ... doctrine of the two kingdoms *separate* until Judgment Day will again and again face that colon of the always open question: *Quis judicabit? Quis interpretabitur?* Who decides *in concreto* for man, creaturely acting in his own right, on the question of what is spiritual and what is worldly and how it stands with the *res mixtae*, which are in the interim, as it were, between the Coming and the Second Coming of the Lord, forming the existence of this spiritual-worldly, spiritual-temporal twin-being that is *man*?[117]

As he makes clear in the passage above, Schmitt always believed this "great" question (of Thomas Hobbes) could only be solved in a *decisionist* manner. But this means—not only in my understanding—that it can only be solved by whichever is the higher power, indeed by *violent force*. Certainly, not only have popes banished emperors "by means of" their key power; equally emperors have appointed and disposed of popes, claiming for themselves the role of "vicarius Dei." Conversely, not only have emperors gone to war bearing "the Banner of Constantine"; so have popes, unambiguously, as "epigones" of the imperators.[118] They too were Constantinian-gifted, Contantinian-burdened.

Schneider aptly speaks of pope and emperor as the "two powers fitted into one another";[119] it is therefore "law" for them to be each other's "enemies":[120] enemy *brothers* who quarrel about their inheritance, which is doubled, and is called: Roman Christianity, or rather: "Christian Rome." This city lives "in the name of the Cross ... and the name of the imperators";[121] and because of that it is an *impossibility*: "The inheritance of Rome eternally conflicts with the inheritance of Christ."[122] But Schneider writes this only to affirm the conflict as the *tragedy* of the "Christian Rome": "Behind the pope's throne dawns the shadow of Caesar; but Caesar's shadow followed

---

117. Schmitt, *Politische Theologie II*, 107.

118. Reinhold Schneider, *Innozenz der Dritte* (Munich: Deutscher Taschenbuch Verlag, 1963), 36.

119. Reinhold Schneider, *Kaiser Lothars Krone: Leben und Herrschaft Lothars von Supplinburg* (Leipzig: Insel–Verlag, 1937), 140.

120. Reinhold Schneider, *Innozenz und Franziskus* (Wiesbaden: Insel–Verlag, 1952), 121.

121. Reinhold Schneider, *Innozenz der Dritte*, 11.

122. Ibid., 10.

the emperors too ... The Christian and world-historical task of *both* was ... to wrestle with this shadow until the end of time *and* always afresh ... on their thrones to grab the Cross and with its help force back the shadow."[123]

This shared "Christian and world-historical task" connects them by making them into enemies: "Pope and emperor are the unity of the visible head, spiritual and temporal head," but "historically *real* as one [only] via the sword that pierces them, that they *themselves* together stab into their heart"—"crossbeam through upright beam."[124] It is cruel, but, as Przywara interprets, it is the cruelty of the cross and therefore a holy, "justified" one: "*culpa*," but "*felix*." Schneider generalizes: "Sword and cross have nothing in common, and yet the cross often becomes a sword, in order to then, on a field of battle, turn into the foe of the sword again. Faith sinks without power, and power sinks without faith. In the end, *beyond* the world, faith will be victorious, when it has wholly imbued the world and has overcome it."[125]

Those for whom this is necessarily an eschatology of the "opiate," for them—as for the *anti*-transcendent Schneider of 1930—power without the cross will necessarily sink only where faith is a power in the first place: because of one that has empowered it. Rome *was* this power, as Schneider mercilessly analyzes in his *Innocent III*. It subjugated the gospel to its "service," and—as it was "doubting the validity of the invisible, inner value, itself respecting otherworldly powers only as helpers, never as commanders, binding the invisible without the condition of reality"—it set "an example," "whose continuously generative force can never be extinguished."[126]

This force governs the "Constantinian age," even when Constantine stands opposed to Constantine, indeed it is he facing himself; "only" in Caesar's "following" the emperor and the pope may be discerned: "the great enemies that in turns cause each other to appear, to increase, indeed only make each other possible by fighting one another."[127] The gospel is objec-

123. Schneider, *Kaiser Lothars Krone*, 143.

124. Erich Przywara, *Logos: Logos–Abendland–Reich–Commercium* (Düsseldorf: Patmos–Verlag, 1964), 110.

125. Reinhold Schneider, *Das Inselreich: Gesetz und Größe der britischen Macht* (Wiesbaden: Insel–Verlag, 1956 (2nd ed.), 28–29.

126. Schneider, *Innozenz der Dritte*, 36.

127. Ibid., 131. In an unpublished letter dated 16.03.1931 Schneider writes to his companion Anna-Maria Baumgarten, "It [the *Innocent III*.] is simply about the demonic nature of the inheritance of ancient Rome, which apprehends two powers at once and so forces them into mutual destruction."

tively only "one more weapon"[128] in this fight. It is about Caesar's fight for power, whereby—and this is what makes emperor and pope an "immortal pair of combatants"—each one wants to use the other because he has to. That is to say, he needs or requires the other. Innocent III hardly wants to destroy the empire; indeed, it is indispensable to him, because the emperor was to be "his executor," "the strong and at once unconditional executor and defender of his commandments. But because . . . [Innocent] thinks this way, he does not understand the empire; because the crown which he thinks he may confer by his own free choice is commanded by what is more powerful than him, by what has long been ruling him: the claim of Rome. It is as if Caesar were to crown Augustus so that both can rule together."[129] And yet they *cannot* share their power; where they stand, both under the sign of absolute rule, there is only space for one.[130] So why does the pope crown his rival, the emperor?

He wants to use him as a tool:

> Yet as he names him imperator, he commands him to rebel. Because the name only allows for one meaning. The imperator has to resist the one who has anointed him; he has to be the first on earth and crush everyone who thinks himself above him. He will never be forgiven if he recognizes a lord above himself; someone will take the title away from him and give him another. The imperator is the absolute ruler and commander, the ordering one as such, whom armies follow without protest. But does not Christ look down from the star-spangled heavens? Are not the pagan words long blown in the wind? They immortally persist through the transformations, and whomever they grasp will be carried by them in all their unchanged weight. Certainly, the world of the imperators broke apart into this world and the beyond; Caesar could be *pontifex maximus* without relinquishing the world of imperators: he was Pontifex so that he could triumph and rule even more safely; but the pope vies for empires and sceptres in the name of renunciation.[131]

We shall leave aside here the ascetic legitimizations of the pope's empire (at the time of Innocent III, a world empire). A condition of the possibility of an imperial-papal dualism was that the Caesar was no longer

128. Schneider, *Innozenz der Dritte*, 38.
129. Ibid., 60.
130. Cf. ibid., 72.
131. Ibid., 73.

a *pontifex maximus*, that he could never be after he had become a Christian and his empire a Christian one. The resistance against the emperor as a High Priest was the last remnant of the early Christian apocalyptic rejection of the empire. Christians had recognized the emperor as a *worldly* lord well before the "Constantinian Turn," having endured it themselves; hence the "independence" of the "spiritual power" had become an even greater point of contention, precisely after Christianization—at least in the Western half of the empire. And thus the dualist powers, far from forming a "hypostatic union," became mortal enemies for life, i.e., each one as much as the other wanted again to be both: emperor and pope, the one and only pontifical imperator of a *pagan*-ancient Rome.

Caesaro-papism and hierocracy were challenging each other to duel, because neither wanted to tolerate a limitation of their power; both were in it for total power, and this is the way it had to be according to the law [*Gesetz*] valid for both of them once they had entered the competition, according to the Roman *law* [*Recht*] to which both emperor and pope appealed as a welcome "justifier of dictatorial power."[132] It confirmed for them that they needed to recognize no human law above them, no law of another *human being*: "As the pope does judge, but cannot be judged, so the emperor."[133] What judges between *them* is necessarily the sword. Schmitt's question: "*Quis iudicabit*?," when posed in the struggle between emperor and pope, means war.

5. A PERMANENT KATECHONTIC AS MUCH AS AUGUSTAN STATE OF SIEGE

Emperor and pope are the prototype for all later models of sovereignty, that of early *modern* absolute monarchy and the territorial and national states, however republican or democratic. That this sovereignty in foreign policy and international law has been largely lost after World War I has been our topic. In addition, we have talked extensively about the fragility of domestic sovereignty, especially with a view to Donoso Cortés's permanent dictatorship of the emergency. In view of Schmitt this last will now have to be analyzed closer: Cortés distinguishes "between a dictatorship of the rebellion and a dictatorship of the government," which he explicitly identifies with one "from above," that is, existing superiority, power,

132. Ibid., 76.
133. Ibid.

and rule. He opts for a *military* dictatorship in order to maintain the status quo—or for (an exacerbating) re-installment of it—and regards dictatorial terror as pious, God-pleasing work. Schmitt will call it "katechontic," and despite such katechontics (referring to Paul and Tertullian), he remained an anti-*apocalyptic*: an "apocalyptic of the counter-revolution," as his patron Donoso Cortés already was.

The supposedly purely reactive nature of such apocalypticism must be doubted: the tranquil, peaceful, just character of the "order" that precedes the "destructive attack" (of left revolutionaries). Brunner's assessment of Schmitt's doctrine of the enemy as "the pure endpoint of a development of the doctrine of *the raison d'état*" leaves no doubt about Schmitt's Machiavellism (which he himself never denied): the *essential* hostility of his admittedly repressive and *arbitrary* statism. Jean Bodin's decisive influence on Schmitt lay in the fact "that he boils the explication of the relationships between the prince and the estates down to a simple either-or, and he does so by referring to the *state of emergency*," part of which is "in principle an unlimited permission, i.e., the suspension of the complete existing order."[134]

In the state of emergency, as Schmitt emphasizes, the decision "frees itself of all normative ties and becomes absolute in the actual sense. *In the state of exception the state suspends the law*." Or to repeat another one of Schmitt's maxims: The "authority ... in order to do right, does not need to be in the right."[135] And once the state of exception has become "normal"—as in a not merely "commissionary," but rather "sovereign dictatorship"[136] à la Cortés—it *never* needs to be in the right again. Its crimes, as "state crimes," are crimes no more, not even "sins"—if one follows the court poet close to Bodin and his intellectual relatives, Pierre Corneille.[137]

In his *Cinna*, Corneille lets "Livie," wife of Augustus, cry out to heaven as follows: "*Tous les crimes d'État qu'on fait pour la couronne, / Le ciel nous en absout alors qu'il nous la donne, / Et dans le sacré rang ou sa faveur l'a mis,/ Le passé devient juste et l'avenir permis. / Qui peut y parvenir ne peut être coupable; / Quoi qu'il ait fait ou fasse, il est inviolable: / Nous lui devons

---

134. Schmitt, *Politische Theologie* (1934), 14 and 18.

135. Ibid., 19–20.

136. Cf. Carl Schmitt-Dorotić, *Die Diktatur: Von den Anfängen des modernen Souveränitätsgedankens bis zum proletarischen Klassenkampf* (Munich: Duncker and Humblot, 1921), 25ff. and 40.

137. Extensively: Faber, "Jean Bodin und de Bonald bei Werner Krauss und Carl Schmitt: Ein Vergleich." In *Werner Krauss: Wege-Werke-Wirkungen*, edited by O. Ette et al., (Berlin: Berlin-Verlag Spitz, 1999), 71–90.

nos biens, nos jours sont en sa main, / Et jamais on n'a droit sur ceux du souverain."[138]

The conclusion Schneider draws from these words is inescapable: "Law is tied to the state, not the state tied to law; the highest value in the end is life, though supra-personal [überpersönlich] life; and because it rests in the hands of the ruler, no duty is conceivable that is contrary to his rights."[139] The words of Schmitt's student Ernst Forsthoff that refer directly to Bodin are fully congruent with Schneider's comment: "Sovereignty gives to its holder . . . alone the authority to define law and crime, and to do so without sanctions in the case of abuse. [Already] Bodin realized that recognizing such sanctions had to lead to the negation of sovereignty."[140] And "so it is" "the sovereign," to turn around one of Schmitt's sentences, "who has absolute power."[141]

For Schmitt himself it is also significant that Corneille gives the modern-absolute state an Augustan turn. Via his Eusebianism, or rather Constantinianism, he was not only indirectly but also directly an adherent of the "Augustan restoration"[142]: "The Imperium Romanum is peace, the victory of order over rebellion and the side-takings of the civil war: *One God, one world, one empire,*"[143] as Schmitt sympathetically summarizes (not only) "the peace- and order-loving" Bishop Eusebius of Caesarea's view on things. Like the late antique court theologian he reflects not for a single moment on the fact that Augustus was a *party* in this civil war and that he "ended" it in a way that was partisan as much as it was terrorist.[144] For the Eusebius *redivivus* "the Roman emperor Augustus" equally and "certainly belongs to the Christian history of salvation."[145] For Schmitt (going beyond Eusebius but referring to the other church father Tertullian) he and his descendants are prototypical "katechons" (as I have already hinted).

---

138. Cited in Reinhold Schneider, *Corneilles Ethos in der Ära Ludwigs XI: Eine Studie* (Baden-Baden: H. Bühler, [1947]), 86–87.

139. Ibid., 87.

140. Ernst Forsthoff, *Der Staat der Industriegesellschaft: Dargestellt am Beispiel der Bundesrepublik Deutschland* (Munich: Beck 1971), 12.

141. Schmitt-Dorotić, *Die Diktatur*, 27.

142. Cf. Schmitt, *Politische Theologie II*, 49–50 n. 2.

143. Ibid., 80–81.

144. A classic now as ever: Ronald Syme, *Die römische Revolution* [The Roman Revolution] (Stuttgart: Klett, 1957).

145. Schmitt, *Politische Theologie II*, 82.

Political Demonology

Tertullian (ca. 160–ca. 220) sought a "power" that "holds back the end and suppresses the evil one. This is the *kat-echon* of the mysterious passage in Paul's Second Letter to the Thessalonians." And Tertullian then, anticipating his descendants, of course found it in the Roman Empire. *Per translationem imperii* "the medieval empire of the German rulers" then understood itself "historically as the katechon."[146] And succeeding them were the sovereign states of modernity, which—as Hobbes could have formulated—"held back" the end that threateningly stood at the door in the wars of religion, by ending the *bellum omnium contra omnes* through a forced peace.

Hobbes at least wanted to understand it as so perfect that *all* eschatology would end in it: for him the utopia of the "heavenly kingdom" does not even continue to exist as a possibility of escape from organized obedience, but rather is taken to function to stimulate obedience: "The Kingdom of God is closed only for sinners, that is those who have not shown the obedience owed to the [state's] laws." Obedience is the condition to enter the Kingdom of God, which dissolves without residue into this condition. The chapter in the *Leviathan* devoted to it does not even talk about it anymore, but—as its heading says—talks "Of What Is Necessary for a Man's Reception into the Kingdom of Heaven":[147] it is "obedience."

6. PRO-ROMAN ANTI-JUDAISM AND ANTI-CHRISTIANITY, IN PARTICULAR CARL SCHMITT'S

The Kingdom is here; it is the "Leviathan," the "mortal god" that—an unmissable signal—in Judaism had become the "symbol . . . of the pagan global power hostile to the Jews," that is in particular also the Roman power. Jean Bodin, "well-versed in cabbalistic scriptures," speaks "in his *Daemonomania* (1581 Latin edition, Book II, Ch. 6, and III, Ch. 1) of the Leviathan as a demon. . . . According to cabbalistic opinions" it is "a giant animal . . . that the Jewish god plays with for a few hours every day; but at the beginning of the millennium it will be slaughtered"—as already Isaiah 27:1 prophesied—"and he will scatter the blessed inhabitants and devour its meat." Schmitt comments in a very contemporary light in his 1936–37 "The State as a Mechanism in Hobbes and Descartes": all this "could be the

---

146. Schmitt, "Drei Stufen historischer Sinngebung," *Universitas* 5 (1950), 929.

147. Hans-Joachim Krüger, *Theologie und Aufklärung: Untersuchungen zu ihrer Vermittlung beim jungen Hegel* (Stuttgart: Metzler, 1966), 30.

original mythical image of some Communist doctrines of the state and of the condition of a state- and classless society that comes about after the state's abolition."[148]

In Schmitt's eyes the Jewish Cabbalah could have incurred no greater guilt than having contributed to preparing such a stateless and classless society. And it is only consistent that he keeps with Thomas Hobbes, who used the Leviathan with its Roman connotations as a "political-mythical image" in the struggle against the "Jewish-Christian destruction of the natural (and political) unity."[149] Schmitt, "the German Hobbes of the twentieth century,"[150] also in this regard followed in the steps of the *Leviathan*'s author; his anti-Judaism/anti-Semitism is, as Ernst Niekisch aptly put it, "a statement issued in Rome's secular fight against Judaea, always flaring up . . . Hatred is driving him, because the Jew is eroding the great Roman form"[151]—which Schmitt, both before and after national-socialism, admired also in the Catholic Church. *Roman Catholicism and Political Form* is the title of a famous work by this "last of the political theologians,"[152] who was also a "black(-brown) Nietzsche"—despite his sentiment against Nietzsche (Maurras called him "*notre condisciple*" without any problems.[153])

Schmitt is part of the "Conservative Revolution" not least on the grounds that he is anti-Jewish, because he is pro-Roman, or rather: pro-Roman because he is anti-Jewish. The "Conservative Revolution" altogether is subject to the scheme "Rome versus Judaea" brought into play by Friedrich Nietzsche, and projective, as it is in general, it is so by accusing first "Judaea," or rather "Juda" of this "deadly hostile contradiction": "The hatred of the Jew against the Roman is the parasite's hatred against the state's ordering power inherited by birth, the hatred of an asocial race against the powerful order embodied by the Roman state, sprung from the secure feeling that only where the state is weak can the Jew live his life to the full."[154]

148. Carl Schmitt, "Der Staat als Mechanismus bei Hobbes und Descartes," *Archiv für Rechts- und Sozialphilosophie* XXX (1936–37), 626.

149. Schmitt, *Der Leviathan*, 22–23.

150. Helmut Schelsky, *Thomas Hobbes: Eine politische Lehre* (Berlin: Duncker and Humblot, 1981), 5.

151. Ernst Niekisch, *Das Reich der niederen Dämonen* (Hamburg: Rowohlt,1953), 201.

152. Cf. von Martin, *Im Zeichen der Humanität*, 130.

153. Cf. Nolte, *Der Faschismus in seiner Epoche*, 257.

154. Hans Oppermann, *Der Jude im griechisch-römischen Altertum*. Ausg. 22 von Schriftenreihe zur weltanschaulichen Schulungsarbeit der NSDAP (Munich:

I have cited here a sentence from 1943 by Hans Oppermann, who was decisively influenced by Stefan George but by then had long become a National Socialist. Then a Classicist in Strasbourg, he claimed in the "Series on the Ideological Training of the NSDAP": "The Judaification of the old world went beyond everything we can imagine from our own experience."[155] Oppermann, projecting psychologically, re-projects "historically." And the (pre-)fascists' fight against the Jews is largely a war on a (long) gone battleground, which does not in the least diminish its weight. As "genealogists" for whom Judaea is the source of all (modern) evils, they cannot do anything else but to a large extent lead a "historical discourse," dressing their current ideology in historical costume. And indeed so does Schmitt.

This can be said not least about his ruminations on Christian antiquity and of course also about the ones on heretical antiquity—spearheaded by Marcion. Schmitt even attributes a revolutionary potential to Jesus' crucifixion, and he does so by positively referring to—yet another irony—the most prominent amongst the Protestant "New political theologians" during the late 1960s/early 1970s, and so, as it were, the modern Marcionite:

> The Protestant theologian Jürgen Moltmann in a lecture, *Political Theology*, . . . interpreted the fact of Christ's crucifixion politically-theologically, and he said: "After all, Jesus was not providentially born under Augustus' era of peace [which is where Eusebius, Dante, etc. had started from], but rather was crucified by Pontius Pilate in the name of the *Pax Romana*. It was a political punishment" (p. 12). And he continues: "Jesus was certainly not a Jewish freedom fighter like the two zealots crucified with him. But it cannot be denied that he brought upheaval to the political religion of Rome in a much more profound sense than they had. The Christian martyrs sent into the arenas still knew that" (p. 12). This is correct. In contrast, the idea of a "crucifixion in the name of the *Pax Romana*" to me seems to be an anachronistic re-projection and rejection from the modern *Pax Americana* into the era of Pilate. Crucifixion was a political measure against slaves and those set *hors-la-loi*; it was the *sublicium sumptum de eo in servilem modum*.[156]

Zentralverlag der NSDAP, 1943), 14.

155. Ibid., 6. As regards Oppermann's continuous reception of Stefan George, see Oppermann, Vergil (1938). In *Wege zu Vergil: Drei Jahrzehnte Begegnungen in Dichtung und Wissenschaft*, edited by Hans Oppermann (Darmstadt: Wissenschaftliche Buchgesellschaft, 1981), and on Oppermann in general: Richard Faber, "Faschistische Vergil-Philologie: Zum Beispiel Hans Oppermann," *Hephaistos* 10 (1991), 111–33.

156. Schmitt, *Politische Theologie II*, 117–18 n. 3.

Political Demonology

Moltmann is right, as Schmitt draws the bottom line, "when he emphasizes the intense political meaning indestructibly contained in the adoration of a god thus crucified."[157] But this is not everything yet. Already twenty pages earlier, Schmitt has equally agreeingly cited Hegel's general as much as emphatic thesis—it could stem from Moltmann's main teacher then, the left Hegelian Bloch—that "nowhere else can such revolutionary words be found as in the gospels."[158] This is in the pre- and/or pro-*Marcionite* gospels, as I add here with Adolf von Harnack in mind, author of the book on *Marcion*, that is decisive for all the twentieth-century authors analyzed here. And in particular I am thinking of the following passage, which itself merges horizons:

> Those with the deepest knowledge of the people's soul, as it lives in the despisers of churchly Christianity today, are reassuring us that only the proclamation of love, a love that does not judge but helps, still has a chance to be heard. Here is where Marcion appears also at the side of Tolstoy, and there at the side of Gorky. The former is a Marcionite Christian through and through. The directly religious passages we have from Marcion could well have been written by him, and conversely Marcion would have recognized himself in *Tolstoy*'s "miserable and despised," in his reading of the Sermon on the Mount . . . , and in his zeal against common Christendom. On the other hand, Gorky's moving play *The Lower Depths* can be understood as a Marcionite play as well; "the Stranger" who appears here is the Marcionite Christ, and his "Lower Depths" are the world.[159]

In the relevant context of Erich Auerbach and Taubes I have already more extensively dealt with this key passage from Harnack's book on *Marcion*. Like no other passage it proves how *the* archetypal *historical* explorer set his subject into a context that was then highly contemporary. Already Harnack apperceived what Taubes in 1986 would call "modern Marcionism." Taubes was deeply familiar with Harnack; but as well as thinking of Benjamin—and Schmitt—he was above all thinking of Bloch.[160] He

---

157. Ibid.

158. Ibid., 92.

159. Adolf von Harnack, *Marcion: Das Evangelium vom fremden Gott* (Darmstadt: Wissenschaftliche Buchgesellschaft, 1996), 232.

160. Cf. not least Taubes, "Einleitung: Das stählerne Gehäuse und der Exodus daraus ode rein Streit um Marcion, einst und heute," in *Gnosis und Politik*, edited by Jacob Taubes (Munich: Fink, 1984), 9ff.

understood "his work as a 'witness to revolutionary Gnosis'—in the spirit of the arch-heretic Marcion, this most important interpreter of the Apostle Paul, whose 'Gospel of the alien god' destroys the common tablets of value with such a revolution that all church-Christians, be they Catholic, be they Protestant, would make the sign of the cross before Marcion's doctrine, if only they knew of it."[161]

Schmitt knew (more than) enough about Marcion and Marcionism beyond that, but he was critical, even hostile [*feind–selig*], towards *all* non-Eusebian, or rather pro-fascist Christianity. For his taste the conservative-liberal Harnack was certainly still too *"cupidus rerum novarum,"* since in his book, *Marcion*, Harnack is emphatically of the opinion that "this philosophy of history . . . , which under all circumstances justifies the past" has "not yet become the general norm."[162] Schmitt could only add "indeed" or "unfortunately so," even though he may not have known word for word the most relevant passages from Bloch's 1968 *Atheism in Christianity*. Here I cite the following exemplary passage (which is likely to have been partly inspired by Benjamin's Thesis XV, "On the Concept of History"):

> Jesus' birth . . . took place in the year zero. Interpreted in a Marcionite way the year zero . . . is completely different from the calendar beginnings set within history and hence merely occur, such as the Roman *ab urbe condita*. Paradoxically one could only recall the new beginning of the Jacobins' year zero, "likewise" intended to be total, its tearing away from the whole "Old Testament" of history as purely the fraud of dukes and clerics. But in the incomparably different, that is, religious *topos* Marcion also rejects, with full *primeurs*, any possible historical mediation before his *novum*.[163]

As I have shown again elsewhere, Schmitt remained tied to the *ab urbe condita*. He was a "Roman"[164] in an emphatic way, coming close to the later *Nietzsche*:

---

161. Cf. not least Taubes, "Walter Benjamin—ein moderner Marcionit?," 139.

162. Harnack, *Marcion*, 217.

163. Bloch, *Atheismus im Christentum: Zur Religion des Exodus und des Reichs* (Frankfurt: Suhrkamp, 1968), 241–42. In an interview six years later Bloch says, as if citing Schmitt's 1970 *Political Theology II*, so in a kind of circular argument: "he who has supposedly created the existing world cannot be at once the redeemer" (*Tagträume vom aufrechten Gang: Sechs Interviews mit Ernst Bloch*, edited by Arno Münster [Frankfurt: Suhrkamp, 1977], 87).

164. Cf. Faber, *Lateinischer Faschismus: Über Carl Schmitt den Römer und Katholiken* (Berlin: Philo, 2001), especially ch. 1.

Political Demonology

The symbol of this battle, written in a script which has remained legible through all human history up to the present, is called "Rome Against Judea, Judea Against Rome." To this point there has been no greater event than this war, this posing of a question, the contradiction between these deadly enemies. Rome felt that the Jews were something contrary to nature itself, something like its monstrous polar opposite. In Rome the Jew was considered "guilty of hatred again the entire human race." And that view was correct, to the extent that we are right to link the health and the future of the human race to the unconditional rule of aristocratic values, the Roman values.[165]

---

165. Friedrich Nietzsche, *Sämtliche Werke, Kritische Studienausgabe*, vol. 5 (Munich: Deutscher Taschenbuch Verlag, 1980), 286; Cf. also Faber, "'Rom gegen Judäa, Judäa gegen Rom:' Eine Kritik des schwarzen Nietzscheanismus," in *Antisemitismus, Paganismus, Völkische Religion*, edited by Hubert Cancik and Uwe Puschner (Munich: Saur, 2004), 105–18, and, as regards pre-Christian, Roman anti-Semitism, see Hubert Cancik and Cancik-Lindemaier, "Classical Anti-Semitism: The Excursus on the Jews in Tacitus and its Ancient and Modern Reception," in *Antisemitismus, Paganismus, Völkische Religion*, 15–25, as well as Hubert Cancik, "Der antike Antisemitismus und seine Rezeption," in *"Das 'bewegliche' Vorurteil": Aspekte des internationalen Antisemitismus*, edited by Christina von Braun and Eva-Maria Ziege (Würzburg: Königshausen & Neumann, 2004), 63–79.

Excursus I

"Nemo contra deum nisi deus ipse"

Against Hans Blumenberg's Political Poly-Theology

. . . the scene transformed during the 1960s—including the renewal of a militant critique of society and the Enlightened tradition mobilized on all fronts, including an anti-authoritarian movement, a new beginning for the avant-garde in the fine arts, and an aesthetically inspired counter-culture [brought everything to life] that the conservative critics believed to be dead. Theorists like Ritter and Forsthoff had just reconciled on the grounds that cultural modernity had come to a standstill. Whereas American liberals at the time had to find new arguments for an unprecedented situation, German neoconservatives had a comparatively easy task. To combat anything contrary to their theory as the machinations of an enemy within, they could get their ammunition from the argumentative power of their teachers. Regarding those unwanted phenomena rocking the foundations of a merely postulated compromise, they only had to name the agents who had instigated a cultural revolution. This turn to the practical and the polemical explains why German neoconservatives could walk on well-trodden paths and in terms of theory never had to offer anything remotely new. The only thing new is perhaps the type of the professor who remains standing strong at the front of the semantic civil war.

—Jürgen Habermas, "Die Kulturkritik der Neokonservativen in den USA und in der Bundesrepublik," 1982

If you were familiar only with the Blumenberg of the *Legitimacy of Modernity* (1966) or Carl Schmitt's *Political Theology II* (1970), you would probably find it hard to see how there could be a question about *any* political theology in Blumenberg, especially since Schmitt was right to attribute to Blumenberg the attempt to "scientifically put to rest *every* Political Theology."[1] In the second edition of his *Legitimacy*, Blumenberg maintained his position, *and* he extended his negation of any and every Political Theology to include the "New," "Revolutionary 'Political Theology'" which Schmitt had introduced in the dispute with him[2]: "Political *Christology*."[3]

As late as 1974 Blumenberg still insisted that "the experiment of absolute instances" had been "run through": "If it is no longer credible that the decision between good and evil is made in history . . . then the suggestion of the state of exception as the normality of the political is lost."[4] But five years later Blumenberg seems less confident, and seeks to counter Political Christology with a Political Poly-Theology meant to escape Schmitt's definition of the political once and for all.[5]

The formula for this poly-theology is "*nemo contra deum nisi deus ipse*," and hence it stands at the *center* of the "Work on Myth,"[6] although it is likely Schmitt had drawn Blumenberg's attention to it; for Schmitt, the formula trades under a "political-*Christological*" label.[7] Moreover, Blumenberg knows very well that at the beginning of the development towards Goethe's "monstrous words,"[8] "*nemo contra deum nisi deus ipse*," stands

---

1. Carl Schmitt, *Politische Theologie II. Die Legende von der Erledigung jeder Politischen Theologie*, (Berlin: Duncker and Humblot, 1970), 124.

2. Cf. Hans Blumenberg, *Säkularisierung und Selbstbehauptung: Erweiterte und überarbeitete Neuausgabe von "Die Legitimität der Neuzeit," erster und zweiter Teil* (Frankfurt: Suhrkamp, 1974), 103–18; as well as Richard Faber, "Von der *Erledigung jeder Politischen Theologie* zur Konstitution Politischer Polytheologie," in *Der Fürst dieser Welt: Carl Schmitt und die Folgen*, edited by Jacob Taubes (Munich: Fink, 1983), 85ff.

3. Schmitt, *Politische Theologie* II, 123–24.

4. Blumenberg, *Säkularisierung und Selbstbehauptung*, 105.

5. Cf. Faber, op. cit., Ch. 3.

6. Blumenberg, *Arbeit am Mythos* (Frankfurt: Suhrkamp, 1979).

7. Cf. Schmitt, *Politische Theologie II*, 123.

8. Blumenberg, *Arbeit am Mythos*, 31.

"Nemo contra deum nisi deus ipse"

Goethe's fragment *Prometheus*, that is, an also stasiological[9] and hence Christological text. Indeed, the myth that Blumenberg wants to work off is that of Prometheus. If he cannot finish myth *as such*, then at least he wants to bring to an end *one* myth:[10] the Promethean myth. And this desire has political reasons. For Blumenberg, as for (the later) Goethe, the myth of Prometheus is still the "modern–sansculotte" myth of the Revolution.[11]

The young Marx, who wanted to include Prometheus as "the noblest *saint* and *martyr*" in an imaginary "philosophical calendar,"[12] confirmed this for Blumenberg, and Ernst Bloch almost challenged him with the rhetorical question: "Are all myths, including the one of Prometheus, in need of demythologization?"[13] Where Bloch wants to save at least this one myth, Blumenberg wants to destroy this one in particular; even though he does not explicitly mention Bloch, nor Karl Kerényi's "Prometheus" study. In the 1950s this study had pointed out the Gnostic rather than Greek essence of the young Goethe's "Prometheus,"[14] *and* to Aischylos' Prometheus it had attributed *the* "position on the human counter-pole to the world of the gods," which "in non-Greek mythologies is held by a divine primordial man":[15] the Gnostic "Anthropos."

In the same context Kerényi highlights the merciless enmity between Prometheus, the "god hated by the god," and the gods' father Zeus, which goes as far as the Aischylean-Pindarian salvific *thought* of overthrowing this "*world*-god."[16] In Greek it remained a "thought, " but crucially here *Blumenberg* does not take it any further. Instead, in the wake of the later Goethe he seeks a defusion, even harmonization of the enmity between Prometheus and Zeus in a "pluralist" pantheon, which *hardly* existed in this form during antiquity. But we will follow Blumenberg step by step, setting off once again from the young Goethe's Prometheus.

---

9. Cf. Schmitt, *Politische Theologie II*, 116 ff.

10. Cf. Blumenberg, *Arbeit am Mythos*, 679ff.

11. Blumenberg quotes from Goethe's letter to Seebeck dated 30 December 1819; cf. Blumenberg, *Arbeit am Mythos*, 460.

12. Cf. Blumenberg, *Arbeit am Mythos*, 633.

13. Ernst Bloch, essay in the *Hessischer Rundfunk*, 5 June 1966.

14. Karl Kerényi, *Prometheus: die menschliche Existenz in griechischer Deutung* (Reinbek: Rowohlt, 1959), 23.

15. Ibid., 67.

16. Ibid., 111.

If functionally Prometheus is to be identified with Lucifer—"Both are bringers of light in disobedience against the ruling god"[17]—then this identification has to be understood as "*political*-theological" or "*political-christological*," as the words "disobedience" and "ruling" already suggest; but above all Goethe's later projection of Prometheus onto Napoleon does this,[18] since he, Napoleon, had wanted to put politics in the place of God (or rather fate), "and he had wanted to put himself in its place":[19] a counter-god in a quite literal, that is, individual sense.

Napoleon, who had inspired Goethe to write these monstrous words, may have only temporarily been *the* god who could be rivaled only by another god, but Goethe clearly saw that a *generation* had grown in the 1813 German Campaign according to which—in order to please them—he would have had to become a member of a Jacobin club.[20] Napoleon not only put it in words, but he was also the first to have made them felt all over the continent: that the fate of lives is determined by political acts. Just at the moment of the Eckermann conversation, when for one last time he settled the score with Young Germany, Goethe remembered what Napoleon had told him in Erfurt, and what, despite the experiences after Jena, he could hardly have accepted: " . . . now politics is fate."[21]

By agreeing with Napoleon, Goethe just before his death acknowledges, though reluctantly, that the tendency of Young Germany is that of the times. And—this is crucial here—Goethe realizes more than ever that a dualistic interpretation of these monstrous words is the more historically powerful one, though in his view it is pernicious. Or to refer to Goethe's literary *life* story: Young Germany continues to believe in a general sense that Prometheus is, importantly, the son of Zeus, as the Goethe of the *Sturm und Drang* had believed in his dramatic fragment[22]—"out of ignorance of the genuine myth."[23] But this relationship was not only suggested by Aeschylus, it was also fruitful in so far as it *Christologically* qualified Goethe's earlier promethy [*Promethie*], and not just the monstrous, heretical words. Blumenberg refers explicitly to Schmitt's relevant explanations in the after-

---

17. Blumenberg, *Arbeit am Mythos*, 493.
18. Cf. ibid., 486 and 493.
19. Ibid., 486; Cf. also 511 and 529–31.
20. Cf. ibid., 527.
21. Cf. ibid., 526.
22. Cf. ibid., 498.
23. Ibid., 578.

word of *Political Theology II, in concreto* his finding of a dramatic fragment by Lenz,[24] and he judges: "'Here as much as there', in Lenz's 'Catherina of Siena' as much as in Goethe's 'Prometheus', the talk is 'of two gods', 'of the *dualism*, arduously prevented in the history of Christian dogma, of the creator and the redeemer, the demiurge and the human god, the binding father and the releasing son.'"[25]

I cannot go further into the difficulties of orthodox Christology in late antiquity here.[26] But "by virtue of the idealist postulate of autonomy," "the sonship inevitably" *turns into* "enmity,"[27] as Blumenberg also notes down, and with this he comes to speak of Schmitt's *Concept of the Political*: precisely its foundation of Christology in Marcion's way; a "stasiological" one, that is: revolutionary and hence "Political Christology," which Schmitt also called "New Political Theology" in the afterword to *Political Theology II* dedicated to the dispute with Blumenberg. In reference to this dispute one can state, also according to Blumenberg: Goethe's "Prometheus" is "Political Christology," and certainly so when this "drama of the artist"[28] is read politically—which is what it has been proven to be apt for—and for the Goethe of 1819–20 it was bound to be so.

In terms of the history of religion, the fact that Goethe's "Prometheus" has to be Christologically qualified, and that the monstrous words may be thus qualified, entails Christianization, no matter how "heretical" it may be. Blumenberg correctly notes (and once again in agreement with Schmitt): "Metaphysical dualism is not the threat that arises from the reduction of polytheism; rather, it results from the self-splitting of a monotheism that cannot cope with the problem of justifying its God in defense against the accusation of a world that is inadequate to the concept of him."[29]

Lenz, in the crucial passage of his "Catharina," "evidently" only drew on "Aeschylus' *deus contra deum* in the *Coephori*," but there the words only "signified the conflict of the gods of state law with the gods of familial ties . . . , a constellation . . . of historical succession in the generations of gods." In other words, "gods against gods" in this context is "the principle . . . of

---

24. Cf. C. Schmitt, *Politische Theologie II*, 123.
25. Blumenberg, *Arbeit am Mythos*, 581.
26. Cf. ibid., 599ff.
27. Ibid., 602.
28. Ibid., 580.
29. Ibid., 625–26.

Political Demonology

genealogies of myth, the contrast of the above and below in it."[30] It is the one unifying principle of the *many* gods, whose numbers alone prevent dualism, and even more so prevent the monotheism that conditions them. He almost advertises polytheism, and he does so with political intent, in the same way that he condemned and fought monotheism because of the absolutism and the *political* dualism inherent in it.[31]

To return to Goethe's monstrous words: Blumenberg himself does not exclude the possibility of the Schmittian, that is Christological, or rather dualist reading of the "*nemo contra deum nisi deus ipse*," but he insists that Goethe actually intended or at least favored the *poly*theist-pantheist reading. And Blumenberg's reasons for this interpretation are convincing, independently of the fact that he shares Goethe's opinion. His thesis in view of the position in "Poetry and Truth" that ends the use of the monstrous words is that:

> "Only the whole universe can stand up against a demonic-divine nature" such as Napoleon, a nature "which has the power to overcome each single power within this universe. The *universe* is the absolute that cannot be shaken in its reign by what is happening to it." Precisely "from this perspective it becomes clear how the 'monstrous words' are about equivalences, which are typically possible only in a *pantheon* of a pagan kind, but which at the same time can be trumped with the idea of limit which introduces Spinoza's Absolute like a singular force into the mythical context.[32]

It is precisely this "singular" force that is mythical, that is "demonic";[33] the universe, which the ancients called "cosmos," is merely *primus et summus inter pares deos*, so to speak. In any case, in terms of *political* theology, their plurality is the crucial object of fascination for Blumenberg. And the fact that the monstrous words imply many gods already follows from the lowercase initial letter of "deus" and the *in*definite article it demands.[34] Only Blumenberg translates "*nemo contra deum nisi ipse*" correctly: "Against *a*

---

30. Ibid., 580.
31. Cf. Faber, op. cit., chs. 1 and 2.
32. Blumenberg, *Arbeit am Mythos*, 569.
33. Cf. also Faber, "Parkleben: Zur sozialen Idyllik Goethes," in *Goethes Wahlverwandschaften: Kritische Modelle und Diskursanalyses zum Mythos Literatur*, edited by Norbert W. Bolz (Hildesheim: Gerstenberg Verlag, 1981), 100–104.
34. Cf. Blumenberg, *Arbeit am Mythos*, 441.

god only *a* god."³⁵ It does not necessarily exclude other receptions, but—seen from Goethe's later viewpoint—would prove them to be heretical. What is already important for Goethe in "Pandora" and what stands in emphatic contradiction to the early "Prometheus" is "a pantheon, an organ of the separation of powers—in Goethe's newly favored word of 'balance.'"³⁶ To further indicate this point, all in the spirit of Blumenberg's "metaphorics" (which are "essential"): Goethe strives for a pantheon to create a "balance of *power*." It says explicitly in Riemer's diary entry, dated around 16 May 1807, that is, shortly after Jena and Auerstädt: "A god, then, can only be balanced by a god. The force has to delimit itself—that is absurd. It is only delimited by yet another power. This specified being cannot delimit itself, but rather the whole that specializes thus delimits itself; but not the singular itself."³⁷

Blumenberg is right to interpret biographically; such thinking, later condensed into the monstrous words, signifies Goethe's "relinquishment of the Promethean *through* the idea of balance," which in that same year would find its poetic expression in the "Pandora."³⁸ The subject here is "the mythical principle of the separation of *powers*. But also [. . .] the pantheist possibility of *reconciliation*, which regards each singular being and then every specific power as a specification of the whole that delimits itself by realizing itself. Spinozism is not replaced by polytheism, but tied to an aesthetic and historical presentation."³⁹ But maybe—in the wake of "Spinozism"—pluralism's *conflicts* are also defused and it is *obliged* to collectivity?

Blumenberg writes: "Gods, because there are many of them, have competencies distributed among them, in a system of their strengths and weaknesses. Since originally they are forces and powers, like forces and powers they are unlimited by their nature, that is unless other forces and powers delimit them."⁴⁰ But Blumenberg also writes, wholly referring to the "competencies": "The world is created so divinely that each one in *his* place, in *his* time weighs equally against (balances) everything else."⁴¹ And does this not sound a little too static, even ringing of class stratification—perhaps coming from a general tendency of pluralism towards organicism?

35. Ibid., 431.
36. Ibid., 553.
37. Cf. ibid., 573.
38. Ibid., 574.
39. Ibid., 575; cf. also 583–84.
40 Ibid., 597.
41. Ibid., 576.

"Theologically," Blumenberg at least explains: "The secret potential of Spinozism still shimmering through Goethe's fourth part of 'Poetry and Truth' is that it allows for speaking about gods, in so far as they are 'appearances,' as is everything else in relation to the identity of the final *substance*."[42]

It is fundamental—and Blumenberg does not mention this whatsoever—that Goethe was not least a *social* organicist, be it in the manner of the old estates (as in *Elective Affinities*), or in a "modern" *state*-capitalist manner (as in the "Journeyman Years"), and he always was so in an authoritarian way; and especially so where (in the "Journeyman Years") he advocates an "*authoritarian* liberalism."[43] It is a mistake to assume that this last is only an effect of the "crisis (of liberalism)." Since Hobbes, its father, this is its very principle: economic freedom by virtue of state compulsion. Of course, in late capitalism, securing "economic liberalism" through authoritarianism becomes unavoidable—even in spite of the bourgeoisie; at least an unfettered economic liberalism like national economist F.A. von Hayek's. I'm specifically mentioning von Hayek, because Odo Marquard affirmatively refers to von Hayek in his essay "Political Polytheism—also a Political Theology."[44] This is the same Marquard who in his "Praise of Polytheism" had deplored—in the manner of the old estates—the replacement of "freedoms" by "'the' freedom."[45]

Marquard's attitude towards the class-state may or may not have been so. But there can be no doubt that he was a dedicated proponent of really existing pluralism. And this is problematic enough, because real pluralism, which is always privileged and ordered, objectively tends towards corporatism. Marquard, who has heeded the large-scale studies of "*neo*-corporatism" in political science,[46] in the "Praise of Polytheism," and not just in his "*Political* Polytheism" leaves no doubt that he is interested in polytheism as

---

42. Ibid., 598.

43. Cf. Faber, "Parkleben," 91–144.

44. Odo Marquard, "Politischer Polytheismus–auch eine politische Theologie," in *Der Fürst dieser Welt*, edited by Jacob Taubes, 82.

45. Odo Marquard, "Lob des Polytheismus: Über Monomythie und Polymythie," in *Philosophie und Mythos. Ein Kolloquium*, edited by Hans Poser (Berlin: de Gruyter, 1979), 47.

46. I only mention U. von Alemann, ed., *Neokorporatismus* (Frankfurt: Campus-Verlag, 1981).

"Nemo contra deum nisi deus ipse"

pluralism. Hence he explicates what Blumenberg only implies.[47] Marquard is Blumenberg's exoteric in matters of political *poly*-theology.[48]

Its basic assumption—as noted earlier in the "Praise of Polytheism"—is this: "The modern state of aggregation of polytheism is the *political* separation of powers: it is enlightened polytheism. It begins not only in Montesquieu, in Locke, or in Aristotle. It begins earlier, in polytheism: as the separation of powers in the Absolute by the pluralism of the gods."[49] I am countering this, and so I am also contradicting Blumenberg: the Homeric gods are oligarchs equal to the Greek lords, who are waging a war of (self-)destruction. Polytheism is an "oligotheism," and *because of that* they can be sure to meet their fateful twilight [*Dämmerung*]. Only one question remains *in theologicis* and *in politicis*: whether it is the hour of the *heno-* and mono-poly, or of the commune; the hour of Caesar or the "Kingdom"—"of freedom." If you will, the seeds of the *religio*-political end of antiquity[50] are already sown in Hesiod: *both* his Pandory *and* his Promethy are "examples '*ad maiorem Jovis gloriam*.'"[51]

To stay in the present: as political poly-theologians, Blumenberg and Marquard, unlike the political mono-theologians Carl Schmitt and Rüdiger Altmann, cannot see that in reality pluralism has long become integralism (or rather: corporatism). The Schmitt School, by contrast, possesses strong realism about power, which still does not prevent their critique of ideology from being limited.

The Schmittians too do not see that the integralism they are establishing[52] is a direct preliminary stage of monopolism. That requires a dualist theory of class struggle, which only those can develop whom Schmitt has denounced as "*New* Political Theologians," namely "Political *Christo*logians";

---

47. Conversely Blumenberg extensively explained why O. Marquard's motto "Nihil contra Deum nisi plures Dei," which he put at the top of the presentation version of "Politischer Polytheismus," makes one feel philological and hence Goethean.

48. In a later presentation "Das gnostische Rezidiv als Gegenneuzeit: Ultrakurztheorem in lockerem Anschluß an Blumenberg" it says more generally: "To understand Blumenberg means to shorten him, at the risk of reduction: the 'divine lengths' of his books need to be made receivable for those who only have antennae for devilish shortness," in *Gnosis und Politik*, edited by Jacob Taubes (Munich: Fink, 1984).

49. Marquard, "Lob des Polytheismus," 53–54.

50. Cf. Faber, *Die Verkündigung Vergils: Reich—Kirche—Staat. Zur Kritik der "Politischen Theologie"* (Hildesheim: Olms, 1975), chapter I, 2.

51. P. Barié, "Prometheus und die Folgen: Strukturale und ethnologische Aspekte einer mythischen Erzählung," *Der altsprachliche Unterricht* 6 (1982), 26.

52. Cf. Faber, *Die Verkündigung Vergils*, ch. II, 9ff.

that is, "stasiologists," in the fight against whom Schmitt, Blumenberg, and Marquard are united.

Nonetheless, in 1970 Schmitt acknowledged that "the structural, core problem of the Gnostic dualism between the god of creation and the god of redemption . . . is *immanently* given in every world in need of change and renewal, inescapably and ineradicably." He says: "The lord of a world in need of change, that is, a misconceived world, and the liberator, the creator of a transformed, new world cannot be good friends. They are, so to speak, enemies *by definition*."[53]

After a delay of nine years, Blumenberg partly joined Schmitt in this view, but in doing so he also acknowledged—and with this I aim to bring my essay full circle—that the "Gnostic recidivism"[54] had proven to be more powerful than he had been prepared to accept in 1966. His "Work on Myth" then is also work on gnosis, which has become Blumenberg's metaphor of revolution after it had been Eric Voegelin's long before 1966. Not least against Voegelin's thesis that "modernity . . . had better be called the Gnostic age"[55] Blumenberg had tried to demonstrate its "legitimacy." Now, at the beginning of the 1980s, he agrees in principle with this fellow student of F. A. von Hayek[56] *and* ideologue of the "Ordered Society":[57] in the fight against "the *Neo-Manichaeism* of the established philosophy of history," as the exoteric Marquard had been defining the "Gnostic recidivism" of "*counter*-modernity" since 1977.[58]

This is what Blumenberg's controversy with Voegelin has shrunk to: what the latter has called "modernity" [*Neuzeit*] gets called "counter-modernity," but he fights it as decisively as Voegelin did—although I do not want to underplay the contrary *religious*-political starting points of the two.

---

53. Schmitt, *Politische Theologie II*, 120–21.

54. Blumenberg, *Legitimität der Neuzeit* (Frankfurt: Suhrkamp, 1966), 78.

55. Eric Voegelin in: *Philosophische Rundschau* I (1953–54), 43.

56. Cf. Margit von Mises, *Ludwig von Mises: Der Mensch und sein Werk* (Munich: Philosophia Verlag, 1981), 261 and 266.

57. Cf. Gert Schäfer, "Leitlinien stabilitätskonformen Verhaltens: Entwicklungspersepktiven und Gewaltpotentiale rationalisierter Herrschaftsinteressen," in *Der CDU-Staat 2. Analysen zur Verfassungswirklichkeit der Bundesrepublik*, edited by Gert Schäfer and Carl Nedelmann (Frankfurt: Suhrkamp, 1969), 425–60, especially 447–53.

58. Odo Marquard, *Abschied vom Prinzipiellen: Philosophische Studien* (Stuttgart: Reclam, 1981), 57; see now also Marquard, "Theodizee, Geschichtsphilosophie, Gnosis," in *Spiegel und Gleichnis: Festschrift für J. Taubes* (Würzburg: Königshausen & Neumann, 1983), 166.

"Nemo contra deum nisi deus ipse"

Following Hans Urs von Balthasar's Catholic *Prometheus* critique,[59] Voegelin excommunicates Prometheus as a committed theist, while Blumenberg's analysis of Gnosis is presented as anti-theistic. Marquard has reduced it to the memorable formula: "*Nihil contra Deum nisi plures dei.*"[60]

Because for Marquard the negative principle, "*that* criticism," began with the Jewish god,[61] this god himself is Prometheus and has to be dethroned by the old gods, just like Prometheus has to be thrown into Tartarus by Blumenberg. One should not underestimate such a *consistent* anti-Judaism,[62] but it is crucial that it is *synchronically and politically* motivated. Its subject is criticism, *respice* utopia, from whose spirit supposedly not only the French Revolution has sprung.[63]

Despite all the secularization theories suggesting continuity, the philosophy of religion analyzed here should not be taken as too religious-philosophical. It is, to use an expression Blumenberg aimed at Carl Schmitt, "theology as politics"[64]—so it follows with regard to the monstrous words: "*Nemo contra* hominem *nisi* homo *ipse*,"[65] or then indeed: "Now *politics* is fate." Nonetheless, Blumenberg, Marquard, Schmitt, and Voegelin all affirm "fate"; if not everywhere as the "rival of God's omnipotence," then as the "fabrication"[66] of a *second* nature. "The renunciation of all criticism and the

---

59. Hans Urs von Balthasar, *Prometheus: Studien zur Geschichte des deutschen Idealismus* (Heidelberg: F.H. Kerle, 1947).

60. Motto of the presentation version of "Politischer Polytheismus..."

61. Odo Marquard, "Exile der Heiterkeit," in *Das Komische*, edited by Wolfgang Preisendanz and Rainer Warning (Munich: Fink, 1976), 146.

62. Cf. Jacob Taubes, "Zur Konjunktur des Polytheismus," in *Mythos und Moderne: Begriff und Bild einer Rekonstruktion*, edited by Karl-Heinz Bohrer (Frankfurt: Suhrkamp, 1983), 457–70, especially 469. With this critique, for the time being, Taubes had closed the circle he himself had opened in 1947 with his dissertation *Abendländische Eschatologie*. Under its impression Voegelin came to his thesis on Gnosis, against which Blumenberg's 1966 *Legitimacy of the Modern Age* polemicized. Not least against this was directed Carl Schmitt's *Politische Theologie II*, dated 1970, to which Blumenberg then replied in 1974 and 1979. Taubes polemicizes against Blumenberg's and Marquard's "Enlightened polytheism" of the years 1979–82.

63. Cf. Reinhart Koselleck, *Kritik und Krise: Eine Studie zur Pathogenese der bürgerlichen Welt* (Frankfurt: Suhrkamp, 1973), as well as Odo Marquard, *Abschied vom Prinzipiellen*, 39–66.

64. Blumenberg, *Säkularisierung und Selbstbehauptung*, 113.

65. Cf. Schmitt, *Politische Theologie II*, 126.

66. Marquard, *Abschied vom Prinzipiellen*, 67.

idolatry of nature"[67] converge, as Walter Benjamin noted in his essay "Elective Affinities." Blumenberg does not mention him, neither does he mention the *Dialectic of the Enlightenment*, even though the turn to polytheist myth[68] targets that contemporary critique of myth.

This last was, as is known, motivated by anti-fascism. But today anti-fascism is suspect—a suspicion that extends even to those who diagnose fascism . . . even to the point that it is supposed to be the fault of the diagnosticians themselves, i.e., the "critics."[69] For the neo-*conservatives* the year 1933 is no longer the *annus horribilis* in German history, but 1968.[70] My thesis is that Blumenberg, under the long-term effects of this traumatic "finishing with every political theology," moved on to constitute a Political *Poly*-Theology.

The "trend reversal" is a counter-revolt that grows into a colossal counter-revolution, already having confirmed the ambitions of the "cultural revolution." Undeniably he relates himself to the classic, to Metternich's *restoration*; central for Blumenberg's argument in *Work on Myth* is this passage from Goethe's letter dated 11 May 1820 to Zelter: The early Prometheus "would be very welcome, as a gospel, to our revolutionary youth, and the High Commissions of Berlin and Mainz might make a grim face at my youthful caprices."[71]

---

67. Walter Benjamin, "Goethes Wahlverwandschaften," in: Benjamin, *Gesammelte Schriften* (Frankfurt: Suhrkamp, 1974), vol. I, 1, 149.

68. Cf. Jacob Taubes, "Wende zum Mythos," *Merkur* 11 (1982), 1122–28.

69. I am referring to several presentations given at an academic congress on the occasion of the fiftieth anniversary of the national–socialist "Seizure of Power" in January 1983 in Berlin.

70. Cf. also Helmut Dubiel, "Neue alte Politik: Falsche Antworten auf richtige Fragen—der neokonservative Salto mortale," *Freibeuter* 18 (1983), 45–63, esp. 50–63.

71. Goethe cited after Blumenberg, *Arbeit am Mythos*, 460.

Excursus II

The Cock

A contribution to the political-theological heraldry of the Bible and its re-writings

In Basel once the magistrate
Had thrown a cock to city prison,
The cock had done a deed which had
the smell of Beelzebub's own kitchen.

Contrary to nature he had
Laid an egg—oh spiteful of the Lord!
The cock—a sacrilege on top of that—
Was as repentant as a wooden board.

So he was put on trial,
Questioned, tortured, and then damned,
And, rightly so, before all eyes,
A stack of wood beneath its feet inflamed.

The cock crowed pitifully: "Cock-a-doodle-dee!"
The Basel crowds broke into song,
But suddenly, someone's shout: "Get on your knees!
By God! It just crowed: *Kyrie eleison*!"

Political Demonology

This is Christian Morgenstern's poem "The Cock,"[1] as critical of religion as it is comical. This cockerel was, it seems, also proud, spiteful even, against the "Lord God" himself. But at the end—the bitter end though, since "pride goes before a fall"—it could only "pitifully" screech "cock-a-doodle-dee." And bowing before the Cross, it even screeched "Kyrie eleison," meaning "*Lord*, have mercy." The poem would be hardly over-interpreted if "revenge liturgy" (which Friedrich Heer mentions in view of Barbarossa's tribunal against the city of Milan as it insisted on its autonomy[2]) concerned the *imperial city's* trial of the Basel magistrate against this cock. With his choice of words the left-Catholic historian Heer wants to raise awareness not least of the fatal representation of the Christus Iudex by Caesar Augustus, the point being that the worldly imperator had served as a model for the heavenly one, or—in the Greek Eastern Roman Empire—the Basileus, i.e., the *Kyrios* as a model for the Christos. Indeed, thinking in particular of the Kyrios, one might ask whether the glorification or "lord"-ification of Jesus of Nazareth had not in some ways already begun in the New Testament. At first of course its "Kyrios" Christos completely functions as a counter-ruler or counter-lord—the "Imperator" Christ of an early translation of St. John's Revelation still has to be understood analogously. But then, at the latest, the Constantinian development made converge, or even had a tendency to identify, what had previously conflicted with each other to the point of mutual exclusion.

One of the many fascinating moments of Herman Melville's short story "Cock-A-Doodle-Doo! or, The Crowing of the Nobel Cock Beneventano"—an emphatic example of (literary) joke, (social) satire, (humane) irony and deeper (political-theological) significance—is that its "noble" titular cock is characterized as follows: "A cock, more like a golden eagle than a cock. A cock, more like a field marshal than a cock. A cock, more like Lord Nelson with all his glittering arms on, standing on the Vanguard's quarter-deck going into battle, than a cock. A cock, more like the Emperor Charlemagne in his robes at Aix-la-Chapelle, than a cock."

---

1. In e.g., Christian Morgenstern, *Alle Galgenlieder* (Frankfurt am Main: Insel, 1975), originally published in 1905.

2. Cf. Richard Faber, "'Geschichte ist Gegenwart': Die Tragödie des Heiligen Römischen Reiches, die politische Religiosität des Dritten Reiches und der Aufgang Europas, Mutter der Revolution, in der Sicht eines Offenen Humanismus." In *Offener Humanismus zwischen den Fronten des Kalten Krieges: Über den Universalhistoriker, politischen Publizisten und religiösen Essayisten Friedrich Heer*, edited by Richard Faber (Würzburg: Königshausen & Neumann, 2005) 127–150, 143.

The Cock

"Such a cock" was this archetypal cock-crow "Beneventano," named so by the first-person narrator after an opera tenor. Not merely an "extraordinary cock" or even just poet "laureate," who, like the "Great Bell of St. Paul's," was "more obstreperously exulting than before"; but rather, as a "cousin of great Jove" (as it is explicitly noted), he was "a golden eagle." *In that very way* he is reminiscent of a "field marshal . . . like Lord Nelson," even "Charlemagne in his robes at Aix-la-Chapelle." He, according to his own court theologians, was the "New Constantine." Melville probably has Albrecht Dürer's imaginary portrait of this first occidental Emperor in mind, which portrays him with all the wealth of the "Imperial Regalia" still extant today. But the Euro-American poet (who was everything but "laureate") also has his first-person narrator frightened at the "cock Beneventano" as an "overpowering angel in the *Apocalypse*. He seemed crowing over the fall of wicked Babylon, or crowing over the triumph of righteous Joshua in the vale of Askelon."

It is important that, in the Apocalypse invoked here, *Rome* is Babylon, and that Melville sets "John" within the tradition of the Old Israel (though the tradition which takes the land of others, rather than the one leaving the Egyptian house of slavery). Nonetheless, Melville's systematic or rather contemporary intention is unambiguous: right in the first sentence he deplores that "in all parts of the world many high-spirited revolts from rascally despotisms had of late been knocked on the head." Melville, who *adores* the "tribune . . . Rienzi," sympathizes with the revolt as a principle.

Melville, this direct descendant of the Pilgrim Fathers and the Founding Fathers, was at first enthusiastic about the promulgation of the Virginia Bill of Rights and the American Constitution, which had become a reality without the regicide of the French Revolution, without its descending into terror and ending in restoration. The young Melville was really almost the incarnation of the American sense of mission. In a famous passage from chapter 36 of *White-Jacket*, which gained him great popularity, it says: "But in many things we Americans are driven to a rejection of the maxims of the Past"—just like the old Israel. "Escaped from the house of bondage, Israel of old did not follow after the ways of the Egyptians. To her was given an express dispensation; to her were given new things under the sun. And we Americans are the peculiar, chosen people—the Israel of our time; we bear the ark of the liberties of the world."

For Melville, America carried the promise of an earthly paradise, and he considered himself called to contribute to its realization. This promise meant for him the liberation from all slavery and despotism, the realization of the individual, "royal" human being. He was particularly keen to speak of America according to his utopian expectations: "We are all kings here." Melville's expectations were first and foremost formed in reaction against the old, mostly Catholic-aristocratic world of Europe. But increasingly he denounced the bondage of the *North-American* industry, and above all he recognized that—in the New World—the conflict between aristocracy and bourgeoisie had transformed.

The critique of industry, as it can be found mainly in "Paradise of Bachelors and Tartarus of Maids," is articulated as a critique of *slavery*: "Machinery—that vaunted slave of humanity—here stood menially served by human beings, who served mutely and cringingly as the slave serves the Sultan." At the same time Melville's critique makes use of religious, mainly Gnostic metaphors, as the title "*Tartarus* of Maids" already indicates. In *White-Jacket* a ship's chaplain is criticised as follows:

> He was particularly hard upon the Gnostics and Marcionites of the second century of the Christian era; but he never, in the remotest manner, attacked the everyday vices of the nineteenth century, as eminently illustrated in our man-of-war world. Concerning drunkenness, fighting, flogging, and oppression—things expressly or impliedly prohibited by Christianity—he never said aught. But the most mighty Commodore and Captain sat before him; and in general, if, in a monarchy, the state forms the audience of the church, little evangelical piety will be preached.

Melville himself recurs to the Gnostics *in order to* apply their critique of the world to state and society; and especially so in "Poor Man's Pudding and Rich Man's Crumbs" (a story closely related to "Tartarus of Maids"): the object of this satire is the "wonderful world" concept of the "poet Blandmour," who claims "that the blessed almoner, Nature, is in all things beneficent; and not only so, but considerate in her charities, as any discreet human philanthropist might be." It is immediately obvious that Melville acerbically mocks the philanthropy of *the rich*, especially since Blandmour—just as others presuppose the "self-healing powers" of the market—believes in the self-healing powers of nature; that "through kind Nature, the poor, out of their very poverty, extract comfort."

"Kind Nature" and the good "Lord" invoked previously: they are the declared enemy of Gnosis, and equally of Melville, who makes *metaphorical* use of their *topoi*. Of course it presupposes that historical *reality* increasingly looks like the Gnostic world prison; "Israel Potter," who was "well-named—bondsman in the English Egypt," and as such, without glossing it over, "a prisoner" for "the best part of his life."

One can also think of Melville's doppelganger *Redburn*, to whom the world became strange when he had to leave his own world of home: ". . . I felt *thrust out of* the world." It was merely a matter of consistency, also in a Gnostic sense and wholly in the tradition of the rebellious arch-Yankee Israel Potter, that in *Redburn* "the devil . . . then mounted up from my soul, and spread over my frame"—to the point of "insanity." Melville's own "spiteful" motto could also be: "Let the world and all aboard of it go to pot. Do you be jolly, and never say die! What's the world compared to you? What is it, anyhow, but a lump of loam? Do you be jolly!"[3]

Nonetheless, this maxim and the "far, deep, intense longings for release" must never become fundamentalist or occult. The biblical reference must retain a *political* connotation, as it says elsewhere in *Cock-A-Doodle-Doo! or, The Crowing of the Nobel Cock Beneventano*, which I just apostrophized again. There, as we know, the cock is compared to an "overpowering angel in the Apocalypse": "He seemed crowing over the fall of wicked Babylon, or crowing over the triumph of righteous Joshua in the vale of Askelon." In this case what holds is Benjamin Franklin's maxim in *Israel Potter*: "God helps them that help themselves." Indeed, in some circumstances the question not only (rhetorical) is: "What's the world compared to you?," but it is also the question of Ahab, the rebel against the world *and* God: "What is God compared to you, devil?"

Ahab the paranoiac, however (in line with his Old Testament name in 1 Kings 16:29–33), is conceptualized as such an ambivalent figure that, in the struggle against the "malignity which has been from the beginning," embodied by the white whale, the "God incarnated"—the godless world or its divine "tyrant," he himself uses "devils" and becomes a cannibalistic shark; he dies with the feeling that "my topmost greatness lies in my topmost grief." Ahab's idiosyncrasy, having bid farewell to everything social, by no means draws Melville's sympathies, but the rebel who asks whom he would obey does. Equally the arch-Yankee Israel Potter has "*no* king," saying that as a Republican of course, and hence a *social* utopian: "I was not born a serf, and will not live a slave!"[4]

---

3. *Translators' note: collage from: *Cock-A-Doodle-Doo! or, The Crowing of the Nobel Cock Beneventano*.

4. *Translators' note: collage from: Melville, *White-Jacket*.

Israel, imprisoned in England, believes he can locate his island Utopia as a "far Canaan beyond the sea" in the United States. The young Melville still believed that freedom had already been victorious in his county. Later he understood that the presumption of a *salus praesens* is the worst possible ideology—though without betraying the utopia. Like Israel Potter he continues to await the day that is yet "to come." Already *White-Jacket* closed with the words: ". . . and though long ages should elapse, and leave our wrongs unredressed, yet, shipmates and world-mates! let us never forget, that, 'Whoever afflict us, whatever surround, Life is a voyage that's homeward-bound!'"

No doubt this is a *temporally* distant, if not altogether alien, but in every case "Gnostic" home. Most importantly, this implies that Melville—in contrast to Ahab, for example—was pessimistic only about the status quo, but as for himself, as a champion of the principle of rebellion, he was also a representative of *the principle of hope*. It is impossible to elaborate this any further here. But at least the question of all questions should be asked: What is the relationship of Melville's modern-Marcionite cock to the one that crowed after Peter had denied Jesus three times (Matt 26:74)? In light of the mandated shortness I refer to Part I above, "Humilitas qua Sublimitas: Erich Auerbach's sociology of literary religion in the context of modern Marcionism."

The most relevant is the section "Auerbach, Bloch (Harnack) and Taubes." This present essay is an homage (hardly to "Doctor Martinus," but) to my friend Martin Leutzsch. In previous times one would have said "brother," and later "comrade": from the 1960s to the 1980s of the twentieth century this "Red Cock" of the Evangelical Student Communities tried to be not a flag in the wind (on church bell towers such as Cleversulzbach), but the connection of the Confessing Church's cock-crow with the young Karl Marx's "Gallic" rooster. Already Melville in the "Cock-A-Doodle-Doo" story had said that the crows of the "cock of all cocks" had risen "like a full orchestra of the cocks of all nations": as a global, or indeed "apocalyptic" crowing. And what did it say, "Christmas-like" only in appearance? I quote Melville: "Don't be afraid." Or then even the New Testament, and there also Luke 2:10: "Have no fear."

www.ingramcontent.com/pod-product-compliance
Lightning Source LLC
Chambersburg PA
CBHW031503160426
43195CB00010BB/1084